INJURING ETERNITY:

A Künstlerroman In Twenty-Six Cantos

GUERNICA WORLD EDITIONS 25

INJURING ETERNITY:

A KÜNSTLERROMAN
IN TWENTY-SIX CANTOS

Tom Bradley

GUERNICA
World
EDITIONS

TORONTO—CHICAGO—BUFFALO—LANCASTER (U.K.)
2020

Michael Mirolla, editor
Cover design: Allen Jomoc Jr.
Interior layout: Jill Ronsley, suneditwrite.com
Front cover image: *Laughing Child*, Frans Hals
Guernica Editions Inc.
287 Templemead Drive, Hamilton (ON), Canada L8W 2W4
2250 Military Road, Tonawanda, N.Y. 14150-6000 U.S.A.
www.guernicaeditions.com

Distributors:
Independent Publishers Group (IPG),
600 North Pulaski Road, Chicago IL 60624
University of Toronto Press Distribution,
5201 Dufferin Street, Toronto (ON), Canada M3H 5T8
Gazelle Book Services, White Cross Mills
High Town, Lancaster LA1 4XS U.K.

First edition.
Printed in Canada.

Legal Deposit—First Quarter
Library of Congress Catalog Card Number: 2019945473
Library and Archives Canada Cataloguing in Publication
Title: Injuring eternity : a Künstlerroman in twenty-six cantos / Tom Bradley.
Names: Bradley, Tom, 1954- author.
Description: Series statement: Guernica World Editions ; 25 | A poem.
Identifiers: Canadiana 20190148527 | ISBN 9781771835275 (softcover)
Classification: LCC PS3552.R232 I55 2020 | DDC 813/.54—dc23

As if you could kill time without injuring eternity.
—Henry David Thoreau

Never look outside for what's required
until you've exhausted the whole of yourself.
—Gerhard Dorn

I.

One early morning in a fecund phase
of my abortive grammar school career,
the local Mormon station went off message
and accidentally showed me something good:
an ancient slapstick orgy, first I'd seen.

The frame-rate proper to such beauteousness
had yet to be recalled from film's gray past.
The psyche and machinery of the day
concurred, projecting frantic, spastic motion.
Since boyish eyes dilate at falsity,
I sought parental guidance:

                    "What the fuck
is this supposed to be?"

                     "Language! Watch it!"

(I thought he meant the printed title cards.)

"It's an example, son—a strange one, too—
of early movie-making. Primitive."

Dad's ultimate was one of my buzzwords.
The other was *heuristic*. I'd embraced
do-it-yourself-sufficiency as precept.
The present poem predates video cassettes,
and yet *Swiss Family Robinson* had been
absorbed by pre-teen me, not merely seen,

its from-the-ground-up ethic got by heart.
Some seven times I'd conned my parentage
to drive me to The Bijou, deep downtown.
(Predated, also, are suburban malls.)

"How primitive? Could I, all by myself,
create a spastic motion picture?"

"Well ..."

"I mean with only stuff in our backyard."

His slide rule holstered, heading toward the door,
Dad rubbed his chin, fresh-scraped (as, to this day,
mine's never been), and hastened this reply:

> Just backyard things, eh? Will your kit be including
> those cracked Bridgestone retreads? Those jugs of lawn toxins?
> That gas mask left over from D-Day's obtruding?
> That plastic crap stacked, blackened, soggy, in boxes?

He always crooned such quatrains at this hour
on weekdays when, enthused, fixing to leave.
Though on his songful way to love his job,
Dad stood me further seconds, dutifully:

> Those aerosol canisters, propane still seeping?
> That engine block sheepish with blown gasket failure?
> That Frigidaire neighborhood kids hide-and-seek in?
> Or simple Swiss Family paraphernalia?

He knew right where his red-haired boy must go.

II.

At this point in our leisured colloquy
green twigs and tendrils figured, not much else,
in sundry self-sufficient plaits and wads
to make, somehow, what I'd produce, direct.

Since banished lately from formal tuition,
I'd self-assigned two homeworks in this genre
of prepubescent boychik fantasy.
Defoe's faux-travelogue (youngsters' edition,
on which the Helvetian *Brady Bunch* was based)
taught clever willow wicker parasols
and veggie fiber headgear. Castaways,
more callow, figured in the second yarn,
an "allegory," insular as well,
yet marred by store-bought eyeglasses, stage props
sneaked in, implausibly to make the sun
ignite campfires for feralizing brats—
a physics blunder, whole-book nullifying,
the hack exposed as un-heuristic fraud,
though knighted, an ignoble laureate.

In those few precious halcyon morningtimes
just prior to eighth grade's copious LSD,
one's educators tended to ascribe
one's pranks to "borderline precocity,"
one's jibes to "giftedness"—grounds for suspension,
contagion kept off kids more tractable:
a boon among inestimable boons.
But not from classrooms, merely, was a nudge,
judicious, indicated. Books as well,

and TV most especially, must be banned
in favor of materials, procedures,
empirically up-mucked in lads' own hands,
by error tried, proved false, or, retried, true,
yet more or less atheoretical.
Dad was obliged to nudge me, though it doomed
his normal jump on workaday's rush hour.

"Question of interest," our breadwinner sighed
and, sitting down, large briefcase poised on knees
for speedy exiting, allowed again,
with mounting vagueness: "Question, interesting."
(Forlorn autosuggestion?) "Hollywood
upon a shoestring. No plastic ferrule."

He winked. But, unpossessed of faintest clues
regarding what *ferrules* are, I conjoined
no eyelids in response, nor knowingly
guffawed. I probably should have.

                              "So," Dad said,
while sitting straighter up a foot or two—

> *We moderns are placed on a wisdom continuum.*
> *You'll need to catch racial amnesia, in stupor*
> *start grappling with things in a staged mental vacuum.*
> *In your shoes, my boy, I would fail before supper.*

He stretched one lengthy arm across the room,
without quite standing up, in hopes to torque
the timely knob upon the door.

                              Today
I can't recall if this too-ready plea
of fallibility by my house pope,

my lifetime default role model, appalled
the wide-eyed, dewy Tommy Bradley, me.
One likes to think a face was bravely shown
to such paternal cavings-in.

                    Somehow,
with boy-level locutions, the old man's
detention (temporary) was secured.
Provisional conceits were got across
through words to this approximate effect
(pretend the following's soprano-squeaked):

> *There's no need to self-induce tribal Alzheimer's,*
> *to techno-sciento-'tardation succumbing.*
> *This auteur's no Visigoth battlement climber,*
> *who's primitivistically wowed by the plumbing.*
>
> *Retaining the junior layman's prior knowledge*
> *and sense of the virtues inhering in rawness,*
> *I'll shoulder the West's intellectual haulage*
> *yet make my short subject Edenically flawless.*

"Daddy," I piped in terminology
that hewed to this broad tendency (one can't
play back as though on mylar magnetized
the amphibrachic diction unpubed kids
once babbled; neither can one versify
verbatim wordage plied, eons ago,
in preterite; nor re-, nor *de*construct
the lingo level Tommy's "giftedness"
in jibing had attained, suspended, lone,
on that precocious border, as fenced off
by pedagogue oppressors; but pretend,
again, his words, soprano still, came out
as follows, more or less—)

"Dances, sing-songs,
free verse simply-declaratively itched
in backyard mud with well-sucked thumbs, Daddy,
and finger-painted daubs of earth-tone goo
besmearing tree bark, unpeeled caveman-wise,
a half-distracted toddler can devise.
A movie's more, um—"

"Daunting? You don't say?"

"Allowing for the outside maximum
believable good luck—"

"Which you will need,
confronting the frank dearth of minerals
and vegetables, of animals as well,
that we could scrounge—or, rather, *you* could scrounge—?"

He eyed me sidelong in an iffy way.

"—that *one* could scrounge from dirt and garden weeds."

An offer to pitch in? A begging off?
A ploy to steer me clear in time to fetch
his slide rule, briefcase, personhood as well,
elongated, into the hallowed groves
of academe, before beloved disciples
forsook the lecture hall, leaving it bleak?

I followed Father's glance, averted now
from Tommy's face to Motorola's altar.

III.

Today's broadcast, Mack Sennett festival
that it was oddly turning out to be,
was likely symptomatic. Some shaved Saint
(the Latter-Daily type), groper of dials,
down-caller of the televisual
electron beams that plagued our salted town,
had gone non compos mentis. His Sanka
was pranked for caffeinated cups, perhaps.
The time slot narcotizing truant tots
was now—yet Hanna-Bárbera's colored pap
was nowhere. Augie Doggy and his pop,
their leashes snapped, had run into the road,
cheap drawings flattened further, waffled over
by silent tires of frantic Model T's.
Fast-motion, from the tube straight to your mind,
see spastic uncles, great-great, yet still youths,
mustachioed, death-mocking apparitions,
gesticulating yowls for disinterment.
In retrospect I'd almost swear the Mormons
forgot to run the breakfast candy ads.
But that distorts my tale fantastically
in what *Das Kapital for Young Comrades*
decries as late-stage bourgeois tyranny.

In evident dismay, my father eyed
some six or seven wobbly-spoked jalopies,
Fords resurrected from his own tykehood,
careering down Los Angeleno alleys

in twining paths, like squads of cagers coached
to drill, such dribbles muscle-memorized
by this tall semi-pro before my birth.

His larynx took a slightly pleading tone:

"How about if you just do the screenplay, son?
Your older brother helped me lay some flags
athwart the sort-of patio, out back:
crisp quartz and feldspar bound with silica,
a light buff hue, approximating vellum.
Their arenaceous grains, tight, minuscule,
point sixteen millimeters 'round, at most,
sheared smooth, are finished much like cotton bond,
for dialogue, slug-lines, scenarios,
a script well grounded. Late this afternoon,
when home from work, I'll school you in techniques
to chafe and scrub a true Cub Scouty fire
(we won't misuse the cheaters you despise),
make charcoal sticks and scribble, crayon-wise—
I mean, compose—"

He knew it was no go.
No lad, American, whole-blood, unskimmed,
would let himself be sighted out of doors
misspending youth, frittering vitality
upon the wussy alphabet. Neighbors
are guaranteed to glance up from small screens
and snipe, "There goes a print man," catcalling
that most appalling epithet: *bookish.*
Less lethal to be labeled Nancy Boy.
What reading-writing Tommy did comprised
a death secret beyond four Bradley walls.

Without acknowledging the feldspar, quartz
and arenaceous this-and-that, I sang
big plans. The ornamental pyracantha
should of its berried branches be deprived
for fuel, melting the contents of the sandbox
(outgrown in any case) to fabricate
my own see-through convexities, contrived
while patronizing no optometrist
as knighted Limey anti-heurists do,
bamboozling all the way to Syndrome Town.

I'll paraphrase our laddy's borderline
precocious lingo, just the general gist,
the spirit not the letter, as above.
The latter kills; the former conjures life.
Pretend the letter's powdered underfoot
upon slick stone, trod half a hundred years
by basketballer sneakers two feet long.
Reconstitute the firethorn's smoky soul
like Yeats up-sucking roses from their ash,
or Goethe alchemizing alkali
with quartz flint in his *Vater*'s house, to brew
primeval matter, *liquor silicum*:

> *Some glass must be siphoned while molding my lenses*
> *to shape insulators for dynamo pivots,*
> *since you've never landscaped* Heveà brasiliénsis,
> *and retreaded Bridgestones, tabooed, are off-limits.*

Our kid's admittedly corrupted mind
could not proceed sans électricity,
thin substitute for metabolic vim,
strange impetus external to the will.

Small wonder. You've just seen his syllabus.
Consider the example of the Swiss,
those perforated cheese- and chocolate-chewers
whose toothpicks, simplest twigs to whittle down,
from convoluted pocket knives, instead,
must slide as toxic off-white vinylite.
Meanwhile, Sir William's yarn, without intent,
reveals a Royalist Socialite, knee bent,
subjected to that outside power source,
Elizabeth Regina.

        So, in whom,
when stripped down to particularities,
can New World boys who seek autonomy
find models for sufficient selves?

        Thoreau?
Let's liquidate that Laius now he's broached.
Him of the merchant's mind, the shopping lists,
tight columns itemized, pinched, budgeted,
with prefab bricks; with shingles, vended, taxed;
with chalk and soap bought wrapped in wax-sealed cakes;
with lime, not calcinated, slaked, but schlepped
in burlap, lurid logos stenciled on;
with hinges, nails and screws, not mined, refined
and duly smithied on the premises,
but ordered in, like rusty prostitutes.
Apparently this Henry's vast repute,
if any, as he ralphs on Waldo's pond,
resides in "timber, claimed by squatter's right."
His eco-footprint, mincing trucked-in sand,
was tracked by teachers of the ilk who chose
to cast me out in unfaked wilderness.
This world abuzz untranscendentally

with such wrongheadedness, is it a shock
that turbines, by default, seemed requisite?

Comes Papa to the rescue: "Whoa back, Trigger."
(He thinks his Tommy's still Roy Rogers' fan.)
"Right off the bat, I must inform you, kid,
that home-made current won't be plausible."

IV.

Thus, with that single, flat saying of *nay*,
one's crystal dreams of cine-salvation
were from the inside shattered, vandalized,
like homeless shelter casements, jalousies
and fanlights by ungrateful lumpenproles.
Credulity is beggared when betrayal
cracks mirrors in the nuclear family's house.

"What is this, Attic tragedy?" I groused.

Just from the way Dad's shaven jaws released
that *home-made* modifier, my *current*
was made to sound ungrounded, hardly worth
the briefest hypothetical pursuit
nor idlest entertainment. Everyone
should know, should have wet-wired in brains at birth,
if not pre-braided in his DNA
when still a blastocyst, barely conceived,
this basic rudiment of common sense
Jehovah lends a newt, to compensate
for stupid newtishness, to wit: to build
a factual generator takes too much
of all that's takeable. Simple as that.
Ambitions of electrics from square one
are infantile. You might as well forgo
the waste of morningtime by asking why,
at least of Dad.

        But quiz your sullen self:
what, in the fuck, is so insuperable?
I wasn't lusting after megawatts.

> *Some iron for magnets, some copper for coiling,*
> *dug up in the backyard through boyish persistence.*
> *Conduction's resisted with dollops, still boiling,*
> *of vitreousness rendered to runny consistence.*

  The old man's getting, shall we say, *mature*
and unambitious—or, still more untoward,
withholding his permission due to qualms
I'll soon electrocute myself. I pout
like tweenies in a grayscale teleplay.

  That pout caused eyes to roll: "A serpent's tooth!
How sharper than!" his body language sighed.
Transferring briefcase to linoleum
from knees that once gained him the stratosphere,
his backboard-cracking elbow half-unbent,
Dad plugged the distant percolator in.

  "D'you really think," he said, "that you, or we,
or anybody, fenced in our backyard,
without the aid of shovels—"

         Defeatist
is not too strong a term. And, worse than that,
unfamilistic. Though a loin-fruit dropper,
indifferent to his younger, yearning seed's
heliotropic brain and budding soul,
this prick was not heuristic.

         "—and, let's say
you dig neurotically till bedrock shows,

and somehow hack through that (presumably
with fingernails), then scritchy-scratch way down
to Mohorovičić's Inferno, child.
D'you reckon you'll emerge, triumphantly,
with all the choice ingredients, metals, ores,
in quantities commensurate to the chores,
so pointless, that ensue, as night the day?
Strikes me a tad unlikely—"

          One's face fell.
Not quite beyond the physiopsychic stage
where tantrums aren't yet cause to call police,
enormous as Dad's son was for his age,
he threw some elementals. Our suburb
abode in trepidation of the din
of hissies from the Bradley domicile.

   "Careerist," slid the heartfelt execration
from underneath my breakfast candy breath
as, down his mile of radius and ulna,
our tardy educator copped a glance
aslant the watch he'd purchased in a shop.

   "—unlikely, yes. However—" Dad made haste
to add (pitched higher than his normal bass,
his protestations might avert conniptions),
"—not altogether flat-impossible—"
He shot one cuff to hide the parasitic
dissector of existence, self-winding,
that ticked asynchrony with his wrist-pulse
and made him wince offbeat as he repined
for chalkboard, students, job. "—that is, of course,
if we're just chatting theoretically."

With ominousness, silently, I stared
at my two nearly stomping, man-sized feet.

"And, after all," too cheerily he chirped,
as shoe salesmen combatting sadness do,
"our home's in coughing distance of the world's
most monstrous copper mine: the Open Pit."

He gestured out the window toward a blight,
a suppurating gouge upon the brink
of my oppressors' so-called "Neo-Zion."

"And all I want," I moaned, "is just a buzz."

"Of course you do, Tommy. And, by the way,
you're absolutely right: glass is, indeed,
a dandy insulator!"

The professor
at this point, gently, heartily, bestowed
a *there's-my-bright-boy* box upon my ear,
and, with his foot-long, patronizing thumb,
mussed up my junior Beatle haircut.

"But,"
he said (and self-accompanied with shrugs
of subtle, stealthy, yoke-wide collarbones,
to ease this caveat into my skull
without raw edges chafing overmuch)—

The end result's thick, inefficient, unwieldy.
Your stator, or rotor, however you term it,
demands vast momentum and acres of realty,
Gargantuan crank, Pantagrùel to turn it.

Or make it a treadmill. Some animate beings
are needful for traction, as you've no hydraulics.
But look out the window. Is our backyard reeling
beneath a hooved concourse of oxen and aurochs?

He waved his hook shot-launching limb to make,
it seemed, an edifying pantomime
of broad preposterousness.

"What would you do?
Enslave and clap in home-forged manacles
some several dozen Mormon neighborlings,
polygamistic semi-sibs?"

I'm sure
his reason (consciously, at any rate)
for mooting kiddy thralldom was to nudge
this movie monomania from my mind.
Triannual signatory of report cards,
he knew that, prior to banishment, I'd fetched
C-pluses home from civics class, and, once,
an actual B. This all-American lad
was tolerably well-indoctrinated,
response-conditioned, trained to salivate
when bombed with terms like *human dignity*
and *human freedom straight across the board*
and *indistinguishable humanness*
of every race, creed, color, qualm or kink—
including even L.D.S., I think.

"That's fine," I said. "No prob. I can enslave."

V.

In those pre-Purple Haze and blotter days
before one's baptism by psilocybe,
one's abnormalities had yet to sprout
like toadstools where a buffalo has been.
I still claimed what behaviorists call "friends,"
who scaled the redwood fence to our backyard
with something like sufficient frequency
to be considered (if one stretched a point)
all-natural constituents thereof,
and thus comprised exploitable resources.

An elegant solution, Dad's slave hint,
to our production's *oomph* requirements.
It posed but one half-hiccough of a scruple,
compared to technical perplexities
with which we, boy and man, had yet to grapple,
and cosmological conundra soon
to furrow both our broad, odd Bradley brows,
enveloping our momless household.

                              Nor
would press-ganging short Utahn juveniles
in numbers adequate to tread my mill
pose any special challenge, physically,
for the likes of junior Bradley, Tommy, me.
I was expanding, busily, on axes
both vertical and horizontal, toward
my present six feet, nine inches. And pounds?
How about two hundred fifty?

(Can't be helped:
a basketballing dynasty, you know.
A mere ten years after the slapstick bliss
now spasming on our trusty Motorola
was "wrapped," as Hollywooders like to say,
my father, in a cage, staked, plausibly,
a prior claim to famed Kareem's "sky hook."
Meanwhile, my Unker Bill, a Bradley, too,
hulked center for the Tuscaloosa Twats,
then, butterfly-like, pseudomorphed himself
into our nation's Next Stretched President
for half a campaign season. How 'bout Shawn,
my surname-sharing Latter-Daily nephew,
the Number-One Cham-Peen Blocker of Shots
in all the N.B.A., who deftly dunks
while on his knees to summon spirit wives?
Don't ask which team, with extra-long inseams,
is privileged to stitch his baggy boxers,
to emphasize clan clownishness and hide
his prophylactic underpants; but Shawn's
grown seven feet or more, costars, therefore,
in Hanna-Bárbera 'toons with Augie Doggy
and Augie's helpful dog-dad. It's not fair.)

    I chose to be no less methodical
or nuanced with the wrangling of jail bait
than with my scientific quandaries.
A small economy was being built:
a motion picture studio, no less.
To introduce forced labor would assume
a source of calories for slaves to burn.
I told my pop (his face blanching the while,
this F.D.R.-style Democrat) that I
would ration if not fatten treading chattels

upon the pale pink casual crab apples
which, from the laden boughs of neighbors' trees,
impinged upon the cis-Bradleyan lee
of redwood slats that formalized our bourne.
Such esculents we'd claim, as per our lore,
our ancient Celto-Cornish common law—
whatever horse shit wowed the Mo-Mos.

                                  This

was getting touchy for the Treasurer
of the pink-as-crab-apples A.C.L.U.,
if only just our starveling local branch.
(Dues-paying charter member was our prof—
though far from comfy coddling neo-Nazis
who, deep downtown, in solidarity
with back-east Skokie Brownshirt brethren, marched.)

  Babies in backyard bondage; young Legree
as heir, if, when, big brother, drafted, died
in Vietnam: high time to wax dissuasive.
Turn back, oh man, forswear thy foolish ways
is what non-Mormons hymned among the pews
that we, hereditarily, were meant
to straddle on the Sabbath (eating dirt
sooner than going near). But, wisely, Dad
knew better than appeal to better nature
or high impulse. Parents, alert, who grasp
the dead contrariness of shavers' minds,
will opt for indirection at these times—

  "I'm proud as D-Day's Eisenhower, son,
that you've supplied the dietary needs
of your—what shall we call them—*employees*?
But, briefly, let's back up a tad, shall we?

How quick would a filmmaker run out of fueling
while coaxing small campfires to wring copper's liquid?
To render raw pig iron's especially grueling.
We've only two trees unexpunged by the aphid.

    Two and a half, to tell more accurately.
Black locusts all, disdained by parasites,
they shed like dogs, and with offscourings plugged
rain gutters with such seminiferous pods
as made the devotees of Brigham Young
revile us gentiles. Popularly known,
resented, execrated as "trash trees,"
far cries from proper pyrolytic oak,
their trunks barked flakily, these splintered beings.
The biosphere's most inefficient source
of rapid oxidation in a forge,
they would be turds, such sorry organisms,
wrung-out black carbon, in short order: Dad's
Cub Scouty flagstone screenplay scribbler toys.
If Tommy is a bookish Nancy boy,
we've cute crayolas for calligraphy.
But let's reemphasize: Tommy is *not*.

One's humbly prerequisite nonce-built blast furnace
fares no more permissibly than one's buzz-giver,
whose innards and chassis, yet unshaped, unburnished,
were meant, from the hearth, to come sizzle and shiver.

One's need to squeeze art out of scratch-built beginnings
(admittedly odd), sparkling sweet with youth's moisture,
like spit bubbles popping, once glowing and brimming,
now's parching like nunly pudenda in cloisters.

One lets one's face fall, once again, this time
straight down the lengthy way to navel-level,
with disappointment, disenchantment, scowls,
so chilling to these dads of future teens.

"Is this heuristic? I think not," I hiss.

VI.

Again from his dismissal Dad backed off,
with supineness far from atypical
in those days of pre-postmodernity
among his child-begetting demographic,
who met with difficulty saying *no*
stick-to-it-ively. So, he kept, instead,
attempting, with fair deftness, to deflect
if not dissuade his more impulsive issue.

"You may pull down and light our fence ablaze
(it keeps no mini-Saints out, anyway)—"

"Thanks, Pop!"

                    "—adulterative though it be."

"What's that supposed to mean? Thou shalt not—?"

                                        "No.

Extraneous to your own topography.
Occurring outside your perimeter.
Outraging ground rules you would legislate.
The structure's been red-painted, varnished, tarred
with Belial knows how many different compounds
bought, crassly, *Walden*-wise, in tubs and jugs.
For Christ's sake, guess where creosote comes from."

"Well, um—"

"From coal, destructively distilled!
D'you think, young Tommy, if that black C-word
were whispered within miles of our backyard,
Bro Big 'n Hung, dictator of salt wastes,
would not have caused, a hundred years ago,
this modest slab of planet to be raped?"

  With an intensity bizarre in context,
he paused to peer at me. I couldn't tell
if his inquiry was rhetorical,
so said, again (for emphasis), "Well, um—"

  "But, let's just say you loosen up a tad
this No-Outside-Materials-Allowed
proviso (your big brother'd say 'cop out').
Consume the matrixed planks that mark our edge.
Yet, even still, depending on the sum
of sequels and of prequels (postquels, too)
the entertainment market bears, might you
desiderate broad stands of redwood trees,
as saplings planted, cultivated, grown
to full robust maturity, chopped, sawn,
nailed up as fences, flammably dismantled?
D'you know what that entails? In large amounts?"

  "*Sequoiòideàe* seeds?"

               "Smart-assery's
appreciated noplace. Otherwise,
we'd both be elsewhere."

             I conceded: "Time
is what, in large amounts, barked forests want
to get their tall selves grown, felled, pulverized."
(My phrasing's been approximated here.)

"You said it, Tommy."

               With finality
of coffin builders driving firmly home
their ultimate fasteners, my pop intoned—

"And time, my boy, is one commodity
that cannot be stretched through, nor fudged upon,
nor substituted for, nor sneaked past. Time
is unlike creosote. No copping out."

"Time's unlike creosote? Can I quote you?"

"You've only so much. And I've almost none."

He scrutinized the clock upon the wall.
Class bells, Pavlovian, were ringing now
all 'round his place of fond employment. Dad
fought visibly the salivating reflex
to reach into his briefcase, thence to fetch
his roll book.

             "Time's no problem," I reply—
and learn that weird fact only as it's piped,
nor know why it's so true, nor why assumed
so reflexly that I've remained unmoved
to verbalize this stipulation (or
sheer lack thereof) before its utterance brings
us pause.

            My father hears it well enough,
and in agreement nods, with likened lack
of due, or undue, thought. Nary a glance
by either Bradley's stolen at the Mack
Sennett-o-rama being televised.

I say it once again: "No problem, time."

Forgetting not to feign another sigh
of resignation, Father looks at me,
unmaskable delight behind his eyes.
Some pains he takes restating my insight,
his boy's new notion, that it might resound
near-rational as possible. This remains
a quasi-scientific *tête-à-tête*
(for now, ostensibly, at any rate).

Slowly, he says, "Time's no consideration.
I mean, not for young sprouts of tender years."

"Correct. We juvies have no sense of—"

"Time."

His roll book, for the moment, is forgot.

"Especially since," I add, "unlike professors,
I've got nowhere to be," and beam a grin
which, like a concave mirror, Dad magnifies.

VII.

So lucky to serve out my preadolescence
pre-Prozac, pre-Paxil, pre-Zoloft, pre-Luvox,
I wasn't force-doped into numb acquiescence,
but bounced out of class on my unpoisoned buttocks.

My fourth-generation atheistic Jack-Mormon
excommunicant dad sent me schoolward, empowered,
my brain spilling forth irreligion's decoctions:
amino elixirs, primordial chowders.

No bad boy, exactly, just following orders,
parentally issued, to torment the creature
who'd quarantine me on precocity's border,
a proselytizer disguised as a "teacher."

It's this crewcut crypto-Saint's sermons qua lectures
from which I was kicked, as a sphincter shoots feces,
for raising my hand, jeering Darwin's conjectures,
and jibing nonstop on the Origin of Species.

This proved just one of sundry oblique ways
Dad's priceless lad was "systematically
corrupted" (not my words), such stratagems
commencing early, kindergarten-ish.
Already he'd attempted to subvert
my being socialized in that dim time
when Edmund Teller, criminoid butt-daddy
of Michio Kaku, launched Nevada's sand,
so lethal, at our luckless, leeward lungs.

With doctrines locally heretical
he hoped to fill my head, forestalling backslides,
on Tommy Bradley's part, to some "half-assed
and atavistic L.D.S. crapola,"
as slid my seven feet of nephew, Shawn.
Two years Augie the Doggy's costar hawked
the faith of Bring 'Em Young in Adelaide,
instead of "earning" sixteen million clams
sustaining fractures to his clavicles,
by Afro-elbows bashed beneath the hoop.
The fans loft bottles at his jaw and yowl,
"Yo, Great White Ope!" for Shawnster brings to mind,
uncannily, a carny's midway mirror
protraction of ol' Andy Griffith's imp.

Beèlzebub forbid that anyone
desirous of inclusion in our clan
should get sucked into such a hellward gyre.
My pop was bent on seeing his dependent
summarily, officially ejected
from Mormon "culture's" prime disseminator:
their public education system. He
would cite my record ("permanent") to twist
my mental arm dissuasively if I,
by freakish twist of circumstance (perhaps
gross overdose of peyotistic bliss),
should opt for baptism, immersion-style,
and, like long Shawn, convert to the dark sect
that spilled, well-nigh expunged, our Bradley blood,
in episodes of savage tyranny,
blunt, merciless, since sanitized, revised
from annals of our chipper Beehive State.

And so my teeth were cut, rhetorically,
in conflict with that crazed and bristled Saint

or "Elder"—violator of the line
which (so I've heard) demarcates Church from State:
that schizo-paranoiac reprobate
who'd got by heart a staggering percentage
of Joseph Smith's dictation exercise,
and who, to keep his bestial self up-zipped
in polygamy's prim polyester pants,
must true-believe no cousinage obtains
between staunch "Elders" and untrousered chimps,
who hang between zoo bars their privy bits
and fling at folks, instead of sermons, shit.

My limited debating skills, so far,
had caused the lunatic to send me forth
for brief durations. An obedient child,
young Tommy planned to frottage sharp rock salt
of Natural Selection in the wound
that was the "Elder's" psyche till paroled,
outright, from formal education—still
the aim of every anti-Nancy boy,
from Huck to Trump 'n Dubya.

                              On success,
did Dad intend to hop into the sack
with upper-crust Episcopalians,
dig deep, cough up exorbitant tuition,
parochially to school me, or at home
to do that chore, as our schismatic neighbor,
dead Frater Singer, did with his twelve pups,
until the "Neo-Zionistic state,"
to quell lawless presumption, donned kevlar
and plugged him on his porch?

Speaking of holes,
the ancient comedy, before our eyes,
now flickered, spasmed, jerked in a big way,
slid off its sprockets, altogether stopped,
grew brown, began to bubble, as it jammed
and got up-gummed in what strange hot machine
old TV stations stoked and fired to foist
their graininess on brains and retinae.

The non-compos-mentis, pranked Sanka-engorging,
most Latterly-Daily and Saintly dial-groper,
who'd started broadcasting this sepia orgy
with no motivation, was rousted from torpor—

—thought fast, acted quick, gave the thing a hard elbow,
got cranking again, synchronized a bit better,
commenced entertaining us two hooky-fellows
with four pregnant seconds of televised dead air.

VIII.

"Um … still and all," said Dad, shaking his head
just slightly, like a lurker nudged awake
in an abandoned auditorium,
"time is, er … as you say, no problem … yet,
be that as may … yes, even if you let
your scheduling restraints unloose a tad—"
He cleared his throat. "—taking your boyish sense
of interval, inchoate as it is,
into consideration—there'll be, still,
one bugaboo, one hard perplexing fact
that can't be got around."

                    "A bugaboo?"

"The sheer size of the energy requirement.
You yoke the student body, all, entire,
of your verboten grammar school. With reins
constrain classmates to twirl your power plant.
Stake out a space big as the block to drive 'em.
That's where it gets implausible: Bro Brig
begrudged your great-great-great (you get the drift)
ancestral auntie saline soil, square feet
enough to lay her down and croak upon,
in violation of the Homestead Act
of eighteen sixty-two, and—"

                    Back on track,
and pouring coffee, oddly, in two cups,
Dad presses on: "—I doubt tweens could grunt forth

sufficient light for movies. I repeat,
therefore, reluctantly, my contradiction:
no dynamo will be practicable—"

   Again, precipitant physiognomy,
my hairline growing stretchmarks—but, before
I can distribute me across the floor
to howl, he says—

        "—or *necessary*."

              One
neglects to register the latter half
of the foregoing compound complement.
One's busy damming tears (or feigning to).
One's straining piteously for any means
to clutch the crumbs of one's aborted brainchild,
one's shattered sense of self-esteem (that, too).
One hiccoughs, stalwartly—

        "Well, gee-whiz, Pop.
How 'bout a wet cell? 'Elder' rigged one up
in pseudo-science class."

      (Such tinkering,
unimplicated cosmologically,
the "Neo-Zion" Board of Education
had deemed permissible.)

      Budgets of salt
for such gizmos come all but ready-made.
Glance out the window at my blighted place
of coming into being. Anglo townsmen,
with hands, forearms and faces of Essenes,

squeak past in cars, fresh off the dealer's lot,
their undercarriages jaundiced with rot.
Chloride of sodium's white ionic compound
can be maintained in ample stocks: just knock,
subséquent to attenuated rains,
deposits off the flagstones.

                Through a throat
impacted with twelve monumental tons
of patience, Dad replies, "Let's dialogue
awhile on that, 'kay?"

                (Such a barbarous verb
betrays, in being uttered, flusterment.)

   He feels obliged, just like the nurturer
of upper-middle competence that he
is turning out to be, to tutor me
on what's real darling 'bout my idiocies
before bestowing on them, gingerly,
the trashing they so abjectly deserve.

   "It's true (and you've displayed a deal of gumption
by learning this before your due suspension)
solution, salty, will be needful, yes,
if we're to jerry-rig a wet cell. But—"

   "So bountiful with unheuristic *buts*,"
I grumble.

                "—'overblown' is not the word.
Its spread would even dwarf your turbine's sprawl:
a continental battery. Am I deaf,
or did you stipulate *just the backyard*?

I thought we were restricted spatially,
not flinging fragments of our half-assed garden
across the hellish, dead—"

"'Elder,'" I whinge,
"would say one simmers over there—"

I fan
my forearm window-ward, but not, like Dad,
to indicate the copper pit that kills,
defoliates bald hills on the horizon—
the dead sea, rather, its reflecting pool.
Both suppurate beneath their common shroud
of sulfur particles.

"The Great Salt Lake's
not continent-dimensioned. Its causeway
bisects the puddle in unequal halves
of disparate salinity, which makes—"

"—it generate one thirty-thousandth volt
per annum. Splendid picture quality
wet cells can muster. Talk about *film noir*.
Your teacher's got his waxed, white-sidewalled head
wedged up his sea gull-worshipping—"

Smoke time.
Being the most emphatically non-Utahn
of all so-called "mainstream tobacco products"
(designed, promoted, as they frankly are,
to captivate Afro-Americans,
which folk the local scriptures denigrate
as *black and loathsome*), *Chills* were Dad's ciggies,
in solidarity puffed with fellow gentiles,

before the days when experts, under-bribed,
let slip that menthol tends to crystallize,
unwholesomely, the lining of one's lungs.

   "Tommy," he exhaled, secondhandedly,
into my green metabolism, "son,
think of a movie. Think, now, of the brightness
that radiates from movies—only just
reflecting what projectors can emit.
Pearlescent vinyl lately has achieved,
at most, fourteen percent efficiency.
Your Robinson Swiss Family screen is bark
from trash trees, hung in darksome slabs. How coax,
cajole and wheedle light's wave-particles
to sidle through your image with the *oomph*
sufficient to be glimpsed, much less stir souls?
No less than two intensities, or three,
of my classroom's vast overhead device
are wanted—just a whole damn bunch of light,
more than it takes to roust my bearded pupils:
butt-loads, and bags, and eighteen further bags
crammed with the L-word, powered by amounts,
proportional, of èlectricity.
And it must follow, as the day the night
(vice versa, too), the 'Elder's' wet cell scheme's
an even dumber goof than treadmilled brats."

   "Magnesium," I whined, "touched off, is bright.
There's tons back there, I'll bet. The 'Elder' says
that, in the planetary crust, it ranks
most plentiful of elements—"

                    "—but seven."

"Or let me, since we're shovel-unencumbered,
hand-wring it from the chlorophyll in weeds."

Although, as adjunct prof, he must've known
sarcasm works but rarely on the young,
and never twice in rapid-fire succession,
Dad couldn't curb his tongue.

                    "Magnesium?
A strange, and short, short subject this will be."

"Fuck it," I said, and commenced skulking off
toward Tommy's room, there to assemble toys
with tubes of dreamy-smelling airplane glue.

IX.

His tardy beatnik graduates, Dad knew,
were slouching, unshaved, 'round the serried rows
of one-piece desks at college; yet constrained
he felt, to reach out, buttonholing me,
for he was verging on the Loss of Son
(back then, as now, a nationwide malaise).
By all appearance warming to the task
at hand, he started talking fast, to haul
his secondary heir unto his side
and cinch the love with ropes of words. Pop pitched
what's called "an alternate scenario"—

"No, no. No, no. Don't fuck it, son. Not yet.
The language, watch it," hastened Dad to add.
"Electrons in their drifts are uncalled for.
I'm thinking solar. Save the Trees, you know?
Your older brother, all cool college kids,
will eat this stuff up: sunshine, not that dark
hypógeal scrap from Hell that needs must melt
before it will behave. I'm thinking now
of healthful, easy things ol' Sol makes grow
(assisted by suburban sprinklers), day
by day, in happy Deseret!"

                    "Green twigs?"

"Tendrils as well, in plaits and wads, à la
the plywood playhouse we three Bradleys stacked
and varnished in a previous, less, um, well—

how shall I put it?—*problematic* phase
of your development. Fond memory, right?
We'll raise a hut, again, but with light seals
along the sides (black locust sap plus mud),
a smallish hole or two poked in the roof.
Assuming we can snag a U.V. beam,
smooth, smutchless, through this Latter-Daily smog,
that should project quite nicely. And bearings.
We'll need some dandy ones. Why? Well, upon
a smooth rotational device we're set,
to follow, like a wholesome puppy-dog,
that ball of brightness bouncing overhead,
while mousies twirl the twig-and-tendril wheel
that runs, in turn, the imagery. This rig
recalls not Edison's Kinetoscope
so much as Jacquard's loom."

One likes the sound.
It's an holistic clickety-clack affair,
in tempo with the Helvetian *Brady Bunch*,
truer to cheap Hanna-Barbéra roots.
It took inveigling on my parent's part,
but, as of now, the latest occupant
of our tribe's social Darwinistic niche
is weaned, detoured, successfully put off
directed swarms of lepton particles.
Forsaking ductile, malleáble things,
I'm heard to hoot—

"A hut *cinematique!*"

The sight of sinews loosening 'round my jaws
emboldens Dad, as follows, to suggest—

"Now, by this time, from dynamo detail
the neighbor kids will have been manumitted,
as in, the slaves are freed."

                On hearing that,
hot petulance relapses. I should've known
a social program lurked behind this.

                      "You
don't ever want me having any fun!"

  "I'm always, Tommy, ready to play catch!"

Pre-wincing from incipient hissy fits,
disclaiming the ungameful killjoy's name,
my pop resorts to metaphors of sports,
confusing me with my sole sibling, who,
in any case, abandoned Mr. Koufax
long since, in favor of the Frisbee's laze.

Reverting to baseball-talk, trying to curtail
his humanist tubers and liberal rhizomes
from roughing the diamond, Pop knows that his curve ball's
flown wide of his rookie's metaethical strike zone.

Coach Daddy demurs with inadequate coyness
to stop our home stadium atmosphere's chilling,
forestall my retiring and dragging my boyness
to sulk in the bullpen like shortstop Achilles.

So, sullen, I glare at the TV, whose spastic
behavior's inspiring my upcoming opus
with traumas to skulls, post-maniacal slapstick,
contusions, barked shins, pre-Depression psychosis.

I'm bounced back to times when the Hollywood hellions
cavorted on fractures before they were knitted,
shared bumpkins' opinions on what is compelling,
and Nietzschean notions that "All is permitted."

Athletics, as refereed, rulefully pictured,
with ninnies in nut-cups hop-skipping for pennants
and beanballs' comeuppance from batter to pitcher,
are limp-wristed catfights compared to Mack Sennett.

My mind is made aware of what both eyes,
though focused, have, till now, unregistered
about these silent shorts: the interest lies
at edges of the frame, where palm trees blow
in something less than smog but more than haze.
I chance to comprehend, precisely, how
south Californian back lots manifested
in parched, peculiar long-ago, when most
(instead of merely many, as today)
made-members of my stretched-out bunch abode,
like Hanna-Bárbera's Flintstones, high, deep, odd,
in the fastness of our northern Utah hills.

One of my brace of buzzwords, as I've said,
was *primitive*, my instincts rawly piqued
not by *Swiss Family Robinson* alone—
Deracinated Family Bradley, too.

X.

In eighteen-fifty Brigham's missionizers
enticed us all the way across the pond
from Cornwall's cold cassiteritic mines
(right angles at the waist, to fold our spines
into the shafts, we stooped), only to kick
our asses from their midst immediately,
out of The Church Omnipotent, suspend,
expel us like so many gifted kids.
They chased us naked to that wilderness
oppressor Feds are pleased, officially,
to label "Primitive," where no laws say
whatever's unclassed Homo sapiens
cannot be shot, trapped, stabbed unmercifully
if it's unworshipped by the indigenes;
but one must eat it up, entire, thymus
and pancreas included, which we did.
We howled at moons, shat like Neanderthals,
and interbred for generations, two
or three, or maybe four. (Spouses and sprogs
are difficult of differentiation
in lightless Rocky Mountain cavern-pits,
where genealogy remains unscribbled,
and selves are self-created, still, again.)

Unlike Mr. Thoreau, who lounged back east
indulging his twee camp-out at the time,
we did not hear *the rattle of railroad cars,*
now dying, then reviving like the beat
of partridges. No, rabid timber wolves

and grizzlies grown three quarters of a ton,
ten yards beyond our chafed, scrubbed charcoal fire,
ripped out their mutual throats and sprayed us red.
Nor were there choo-choos beating partridge-wise
within a thousand miles of our exile,
in that dim age before the Golden Spike,
by cinching Trade's metallic ligature,
garrotted our Edenic Occident.

No more than forty years had come and passed
between the silent screwball telecast
and proto-Bradleys' tentative decision
to gravitate and shamble down from crags,
insinuating élongated selves
among the very folks who'd, mob-wise, ruled
(for motivations yet under dispute)
to run us off like halitotic pets.
The profiles we maintained were low (not short),
unbenefitting from their welfare state,
flat-ostracized (thank Christ almighty: I'd
have made a horrifying missionary).
The opportunities for heathens, us,
to snag careers were few: sordid tenure
among the commies, rummies, pederasts,
free-versifiers, bland behaviorists,
plus slide rule-slinging sweethearts like ol' Pop,
at "Neo-Zion's" solitary, numb,
lugubrious, forlorn, out-stuck sore thumb
of a non-Mormon university.

If Tommy's backyard studio's self-contained,
it's modeled pridefully upon his clan.
That very fall we'd planted Great Grandam
(or Great-Great Auntie—difficult to say),

who could, before senility's cruel balk,
burp forth some dozen guttural lexemes
of private lingo cousins (siblings?) talked
among the stalagmites and sucked bat bones:
Brontës without the literacy skills.
Our kith, kin, blood, race, seed won't misrecall
this heritage of victimology.

   Again, the other buzzword's *primitive.*
It suits my single parent—even him,
the academic with the troglodyte
wedged underneath the tenure-track veneer.
It's sneaking out this morning, you can tell.
Waylay the old man, bore him long enough,
unanswerably, with impromptu conundra,
the sagebrush lycanthrope will show its snout.
Bring forth the Bradley, briefly, then, look out:
instruction starts in earnest—

                "Actually,
someone will need to be outside, won't they,
to turn our dandy hut *cinematique*?"

   From small screen stirring neither half-closed eye,
Dad witnesses a Chassid-hatted clown
dunked face-first in a hogshead, all but drowned.

   "You manumit *most* of the neighbor kids
is what I meant to say."

              "Yeah. What we need's
a yoke of rotators."

"You may withhold
their freedom from two youngsters, maybe three,
selected more for tractability
than mere skeletomuscularity.
Our homely hut's not hard to heave, nor ho,
if we can smooth the bearings, make 'em go.
Envision, Tommy, if you will, relays
of unbarked rollers, utilizing logs
from our black locust trees, all two-point-five.
But they'll need patience, boy, your burdened beasts,
and steady, stubby personalities,
to dog the sun. Real petty bourgeois types."

Our phosphorescent peephole on the past
now perpetrated raunchiness, mayhem
upon bit players, amateur recruits
by some casting director lured, seduced
from Los Angelic skid rows, bootlegged booze
as bait. Their faces' blank abnormalcies
were with mascara viscidly enhanced,
their teeth waxed black like traumas long repressed.
Could I imagine being more entranced
by such collateral Bradleys, hulked and lurched
a little too far west?

"Might I suggest
the junior Saint next door who sports the specs?"

"Those optics must be confiscated, smashed.
You've raised no contra-heurist Pommy ponce."

"His plumpish sister, Whoozit, whose striped cat
transgresses in your sandbox—"

"Tiffany?"

On that trisyllable, Father regressed
to atavistic cave spelunker mode.
Reflexive victimologizer Pop's
sharp upper canines chawed his lower lip.

"—named for the fabricator of *favrile*.
There'll later be a special job of work
for plumpish Tiffany."

"How so?"

Dad scorned,
demurred, or feared acknowledging my ask.

"We build the light-tight playhouse for, say, three:
paired patrons plus exhibitor—that's you.
Install a pedal, sprocketed, whereby
the show must go on, if contingencies
should cause the wretches toiling in the sun
to die from melanoma, malnutrition,
or strike, perhaps, or sap, with furtiveness,
the creosoted fence as fugitives
while you're in Motion Picture Dreamland with—
say, where'll your audience be coming from?"

"You want an invite to the World Premiere?"

"Not necessary, thank you. But, if, son,
you're selling tickets—rather, bartering 'em
(since there's no currency, as far as I,
your landlord, have been made aware)—should not
the population pool from which these punters

be pulled comprise, like pyracantha boughs,
a natural occurrence of our yard?"

   Something is being driven at, to which
I'm too young readily to cotton on.
I choose not to pursue it, gingerly,
and so, or neither, does my propagator.
As usual, a subject of such bent,
though it provokes, feels better left unprobed,
for present purposes, and the time being.

XI.

And now he might, if semblance isn't strained,
unfeignedly be warming to the task.
As Prohibition inhumanity
exacerbates on television, Dad's
unable to avoid, by slim degrees,
asserting him into the scheme:

              "You'll do
all this?" he asks with eyes and arms. "Or *we*?"

   High time to firm the duty roster up,
to nail these pronouns on the breakfast table
and count them, single, plural. Pop's prepared,
perhaps enthused, to join, but must concede
the present project, qualitatively,
will differ from the plywood playhouse we'd
once knocked together, man, youth, boy, all three.
It's Tommy's individuality
up from the ground here cobbled, rigged, roughed out.
Dad and that other Brad are finished huts.
The former's function's but advisory,
financial backer, too.

             And caterer.
I wasn't planning, like my "employees"
(to euphemize plump Tiffany plus sib),
on apples of the crab sort to subsist.
Indoors I would, upon a daily basis,
sashay for several sandwiches or so,

perhaps some macaroni, purple jello,
of hygienic ingredients composed
with funds bought, duly earned on that loved job
from which his bright boy's pouting importune
for fulltime parenting was balking Dad.
Indulgent, kindly, he'd not trouble me
with such an obviousness, allowed to slip,
conveniently, my baby boomer mind.
He'd stay my victualler, steadfast, perma-stocked,
for all twelve hundred eons it would take
to grow, chop, burn my forests, shoot and cut
my masterpiece from scratch—because, as Pop
would always say (and this is not made up)—

"We are immortal."

              When the Big Question
arose (and, with a morbid tyke like me
so hugely underfoot, it often did),
straight deathlessness is what the codger pled.
Not merely banking on the sturdiness
of posthumous repute full-guaranteed
Promethean bringers of such quantum boosts
to worldwide human culture, as, let's say,
the pre-Abdul Kareem Jabbar sky hook,
Dad sang our corporal non-impermanence.
How's that for tenure?

            A philosopher
from no dark depths, dear Dad, who would deny
the grounding fact of beingness, the fifth
perfected state of organismhood,
chilled dread of which spurs much sublime ambition,
plus films of every budgetary range.

Ignoring when not flatly contradicting
this truest of all truisms, up till
his sixty-sixth or -seventh birthday, when
his prostate rendered him edúcable,
my old man preached this poem's suggestive theme—

The Unproblematicity of Time:

Our hometown's boss god, on a planet called Kolob
(that's "bollock" spelled backwards), gets dorked in the darkness
by harems of houris. Why chuckle if ol' Pop
should stake such a wrongheaded claim for his carcass?

It's Far-Western, somehow, not simply hubristic,
to brag incorruption like saints flouting quicklime,
less megalomanic than Jack-Mormonistic.
Our spines are extended, so why not our lifetimes?

XII.

So Tommy's nourishment's provided for
indefinitely, and he's quite content
to let the nearby luminous plasma sphere
project his art. But via what medium?

No longer can we put off trotting out
a certain compound, indestructible,
undead in fact, as, in person, the prof
has fantasized our mortal coils to be.
This needs some subtlety.

                              "All right, we're set,"
enunciates our fledgling *haute-auteur*,
eschewing the first-person singular
in favor of the we-dictorial.
(Synthetic, sinister, what he now moots
with grownup supervision's best abused.)

> *We've manpower from Mo-Mos, radiation from Helios,*
> *but nothing to shimmer our vitamin D through.*
> *The plasticky stuff—what's it called—that all previous*
> *D. W. Griffiths glued images onto—?*

Before our boy can recollect the name
of this unhallowed preparation, up
leaps Pop to both long feet, upsets each cup,
and through the ceiling nearly sends his dome.

"D'you want to speak of primitivity?
Guess what the earliest photography
was made on."

       "A tight schedule?"

             "Plates of *glass!*"

"On blades of grass?"

          "Recyclable, pellucid,
non-leaching, abiotic, crystalline—"

Hyping his counter-mooted silicate,
Dad's being, shall we say, a tad emphatic,
too earnestly contradistinguishing
its sparkling facets from the convolutions,
so toxic, mutagenic, of the crap
now poised to veer and blab from my tongue's tip.
Unreasoning aversion, so it seems,
against the thought of stuff that's plasticky
will override his need to go to work,
and obligation to discourage boys
from time-consuming, pointless enterprise.
What trauma to his epigenome stamped
this prejudice on Pop's amygdala
in our ancestors' pictureless Lascaux,
involving the concoction, time ago?

"Yes, and," he urges, my progenitor,
supportive confidant that he remains
no less under duress, "we'll resurrect
your smart sandbox idea for this *glass.*
You'll have, from the pale sediment, to comb

the scat of plumpish Tiffany's striped cat,
that tidy little beast. From your supply
of shattered quartz must, turd by turd, be purged
excess impurities."

        "Clean the latrine?
Why me?"

      "Nobody said science was fun.
Unleash her brother briefly from the bearings.
Force him to—oh, damn it."

           "What? What?"

                "Niter."

An excellent and brand-new dirty word
burps forth from secret grownup lexica!
A euphemism for their intercourse?
The "N-word" everyone gets flustered by?

"Niter?" I say, no doubt too avidly.

"It's not impossible, one might suppose,
our smallish middle-class rear plot could yield
that mineral, to supplement the grit
for rudimentary glassworks. Who can know?
Unless—"

      He steals a sidelong glance toward
the broom closet, behind whose warping door
our books are mostly stuffed.

           "—we look it up."

In unison, after no undue pause,
novice and master shake pre-Google heads
at that preposterousness.

It's just a chat
between two amateurs with no great letch
for scientificality. Slide rules
in Dad's side-grove of hallowed academe
are plied to reckon inputs, outputs, greed
and need, not unpriced molecules, unbought,
unpaid-for, rattling 'round the cosmic shop,
for he professes Carlyle's dismal science.
And I, of course, the budding "creative,"
guffaw at merest whispers of research.
Thoreau I'd thrown atheoretically
with Golding into Book-Broom Closet Hell.

"So, anyway, you'll have to round your slaves,
thralls, drudges, chattels, servitors back up,
to dig for saltpetre—"

Before I jibe
on squelched libidos, Dad makes haste to add—

"—alias potassium nitrate. Ask, perhaps,
your unfree waifs to disinter a mite
of manganese as well, just half a spoon,
if it's no bother, like Phoenicians,
who learnt the process accidentally:

Returning from rounding Gibraltar to dicker
with as-yet-un-Mormonized Bradleys in Cornwall,
our ingots as ballast in burlap and wicker,
these so-called Red People pay Cyprus a port call.

They're shopping for copper to make our tin brighter,
promoting the Bronze Age; but meanwhile they're scraping
from guano in Cypriot bat caves white niter,
not yet an explosive, but nice for soap-making.

Etesian winds whip a squalling borasco
which radiates roughness, compounding the breezes.
These merchants unwillingly jettison cargo
including black minerals gained in Magnesia.

The powdery potpourri's blent with the beach grout,
and later's subjected to heating at low tide
when sailors set cauldrons on embers for cookouts
of purple snails stewed in the briny blue bromide.

Up-scraped is postprandial charcoal, Cub Scouty,
to roll into crayons for alphabetizing
succinct bills of lading with letters you're flouting
in favor of daydreamt-up cinematizing.

Phoenicians are dazzled, libations once sprinkled,
to see a glazed window, uncolored, unbending,
displaying the underfoot shells of the shingle.
Already they've strategized methods for vending.

"I don't know if they always threw cookouts
subséquent to their shipwrecks," offers Dad,
"but there you have it."

                "Heat? Subjected to?
I thought you said—"

                "Your smelting operation,
let's get it back on line. I've changed my mind.

Since, as you've said, we needn't self-induce
Alzheimer's Syndrome in the tribal sense,
we'll reinvent, blithely, the blast furnace,
as floated by you previously, bright boy!"

He mussed my ginger Beatle bangs again,
and, just like that, by arbitrary fiat,
declared my forge of fire permissible.

XIII.

"Speaking of rollers," Father said, "recall
the bearings for our hut *cinematique*
are locust logs (the black sort), which allows
that much less greenhouse gas to waft aloft.
We'll need to bake a single glassy batch,
assuming we're not lax; nevertheless,
I fear that our beloved little playhouse,
which we, shoulder to hardy shoulder, built
alongside your cool varsity big bro,
must now be razed, its plywood cannibalized."

Far be it from boys mawkishly to wax,
but Tommy had to ask, "Don't you think, Pop,
it's happier to contrive a goodly blob
of that strange stuff I'm calling 'plasticky,'
which movie makers, since antiquity,
have used for—"

"Silver!"

"Huh?"

"We need some."

"But

I thought this was a barter universe."

"Old calotypes comprised halides of such
up-magicked in the darkness, then to light

exposed on plates of you-know-what. Fillings,
are there, among those baby teeth of yours?"

"You pay for them."

           "I mean of argent cast.
We'll pry them loose for halide-iodides.
Do dentists still use sterling nowadays?
My head's jam-packed. Is yours? The pederast
with strong sadistic leanings down the lane
bills me as though he's pushing platinum."

  Not merely oral hygiene's being bandied.
The rapine of dentition in deep dreams,
says You-Know-Who's much castigated treatise
on their interpretation, signifies
castration, patriarchy-style: the pop
attempting (not in consciousness, mind you,
but as a function of biology)
to subsume and to absorb, which is to say
emasculate the son, in full accord
with psychoanalytic regulations.
This proposition found me unenthused.
Unsure what alloys might be packed and tamped
into my own reamed-out bicuspids, I
crossed both fast-growing legs and said—

               "Hey, Dad!
I know. How about if, while they excavate
magnesium and niter—"

           "Manganese."

"Whatever."

"No, you'd best get that one right."

"—what if my schleps should stumble on a stash,
some ancient Mormon pioneer-type coins,
and we use them instead of my—"

                    Shudders,
not necessarily stemming from my jaws,
both still unshaven, shook the last word off.

  So desperate to avoid, at least postpone,
the Oedipally ultimate high noon,
I was prepared to stretch another point:
a century's worth of backyard burial
would render this bullion permissible—
unlike the Bridgestone tires and Frigidaire.
(A mere ten years they'd lain and rotted there.)
Whatever treasure trove statutes sucked ink
upon the law books of the Beehive State
would be dismissed, scorned, roundly contravened.

  "A hoard of Saintly specie?" scoffed my pop.
"Untithed? Unpillaged? Left by Brigham Young,
the greedy prick who had us mostly lynched
for one-sixth acre's worth of puckered sagebrush?"

  "But Great-Great Auntie said our folk transgressed—"

  Two recapitulated Dad refrains
cut in: "Strikes me a tad unlikely," then,
"Not altogether flat-impossible."

  He said, "Let's say you suck sufficient halides
off this sad pittance somehow overlooked

by our oppressors' vast voraciousness.
In the procedure, drastically, I fear,
this Mo-Mo moolah's bound to be defaced.
Will archaeologists approve?"

                        From that
the Bradleys both derived passing guffaws.
They weren't exactly Attic owl drachmas.

   "And so," said Dad, appearing tension-free,
"we've made our contribution to world culture.
Our edifying artifact's comprised
of moving pictures, negatives, as run
upon glass plates, projected by the sun.
So now we'll stop, and I will go to work,
arriving just in time to scarf some lunch,
and everything has settled into place,
and you, son, I'll see later on. 'Bye, now."

XIV.

My relatively little ears perked up,
like Augie Doggy's daddy's favorite pup's.
Did I hear right? We're making negatives?
Flipped shadows whose inversion's absolute?
So, why was I the last to know? It struck
young Tommy as superb.

                This thing would loom
like Death, which, as our morning chat progressed,
thematically asserted its lush self,
the very *mise-en-scène* of my debut—
though, at this stage you could've asked me why,
and gotten shrugs and rolled eyes in reply.
You'd think Tommy a semi-skosh too young
to have mortality upon the brain
cerebrospinal fluid-wise.

                "Oh, boy!
A negative aesthetic would be swell!
Real avant-garde!"

                "But you should be prepared
emotionally," Dad said, while hefting high
his briefcase, "for a picture quality
aspiring to atrociousness: umbras
that, dim and gray, galumph upon the wall.
Real Plato's cave crapola."

"I don't care.
A *Cleopatra* Burton-Taylor remake's
not in the title cards. Think *cinéma
naïveté*, like early *Little Rascals*
before Farina dropped some testicles."

"It strikes me, still, a tad unlikely—though
not altogether flat-impossible."

"Goes without saying."

"Good, it's settled then."

On first-string center legs, doorward Dad lunged.
And here I thought we spoke in principle.

With intonations adequately firm
to arrest his jobward progress, yet high-pitched
with wheedling childishness, I lisped, "Daddy?
One eensy-weensy simple question more,
about the silver—um, thingies."

"Halides."

"How do we make them stick onto the glass?"

"Oh, they're suspended—"

Catching words up short,
he shoved another *Chill* into his mouth
to freeze with menthol indiscretion's flow.
My ears, like Shawn's costar's, twitched yet again.

"Suspended? By what? Through what?"

"Nothing, son."

"That doesn't sound heuristic. Even I
can boast to be suspended *from* something.
Or, are these silvery this-'n-thats—"

"Halides."

"—suspended *in* nothing? What, in the fuck,
are you, in this context, talking about?"

The mutter came—

"Language. Watch it."

—with half
the heartedness of previous iterations.
It seemed paternal *oomph*, a modicum,
was draining off my old pop's will to stir.

Untorqued, the doorknob left his giant fist.
The chair received his buttocks. His briefcase
was sent to arch across the room—sky hook.
Abandoned was his face by easeful looks.
Enthusiasm vacated his voice,
which, barely audible, sighed—

"Gelatin."

"So? What's the heart attack? We bide our time
till Mo-Mos have a picnic, slide a twig
between the fence slats, latch onto a plate,
suck out the tiny marshmallows. Voilà!
It's showtime at the Bradleys."

"That's jello.
What we need's *gelatin*, spelled with a *Gee*,
and not just any gross colloidal guck.
D'you want to know what grownups call it?"

"Sure."

"They call it *animal jelly*."

Father paused
and eyed me, briefly, in the hope (forlorn)
that such a notion would elicit "Eeeew,
for *ick*," and put me off the silver screen,
his child scared straight, once and for all, The End—
non-Mormon university or bust.
But he was raising no Miss Sissy-Pants,
nor Nancy Boy. True lads, if regular,
adore, in all her permutations, mucus.

"Heuristic, Pop! Earthworms are animals.
We could employ earthworms. It's 'tard-simple
to grow earthworms, if you know how. Your hand
is plunged into the mass, slowly withdrawn,
as when preparing for a fishing trip,
then *beaucoup* critter snot gets harvested
for mushing with the tooth-hole plugging crap."

"You honestly have no regard," Dad said,
"for picture quality. Is that correct?"

"So maybe I should go into TV."

With equal parts revulsion and blind fear
enlarging his outdoor voice, he yelled—

"No!
Connective tissue, tendons, ligaments
of vertebrates yield gelatin, not slick
secretions from the oral-anal vents
of writhing, irritating annelids!"

"Oh, if you please, I do beg pardon. And
this nectar can be had by? From? How? Whom?"

"Not every man is blessed with a vocation
through which fulfillment daily gets derived,"
said Father, longingly.

"D'you want, or not,
your favorite, better son to do heuristics?"

"The best source, pound for pound, is hooves. Cow, now,
but formerly ol' Trigger. You recall
glue factories."

"I don't."

"Grotesque amounts
of honest work we'd skip, shamefully neglect
our beatnik grads, and wait, instead, for herds
of ungulates, with odd or even toes,
to stampede up the boulevard and down
our driveway. Or we'd listen for contingents
of their wild cousins clippity-clopping by,
migrating, making inroads, trampling trails,
establishing what's called 'paths of desire'—
a turn of phrase I've always found compelling—"

He sighed and eyed his Ford keys on the table.

"To admit the bringers of our collagen,
a serviceable hole must needs be kicked
through creosoted slats that squeeze our world.
I feel like doing that right now."

                              "I thought
we burned the fence already."

                        "But of course."

I doubt many quadrupeds sporting horned foot-parts
were browsing our salt prior to Brig and his hundred
and eighty-nine wives pulling up in their oxcarts,
their dust aspirated by Bradleys who'd blundered.

Just horny toads, pumas, Paiutes in quaint headbands
and kangaroo-rats, hanta-viral, fanged, furry.
It's desert the Saints coaxed to blossom, not grasslands,
if unfamed for breeding one-humped dromedaries—

"—but, wait, are camels hooved?"

                              The doddering coot's
now asking questions of himself, out loud,
forgetting superciliously to cast
a glance against the book-broom closet's door.

    Attempting to get back on topic, or
at least the proper continent, I jibe—

    "Your bison-buffaloes have juicy stompers,
but they're adopt-a-pets of Uncle Sam."

    —and might as well have mouthed no josh at all.

"Since time's no problem, Tommy, as you've said,
let's wait for one big bastard asteroid
to swing along and punch us both off kilter,
and slide our backyard far, to latitudes
that might conduce to jelliable beasts,
such as Brazil. I always thought tapirs
would make nice amber-colored photo sauce."

His brain's gauzing. Maturity forebodes.
The day is due, perhaps too soon, when I
will have, to this old soul, bid fond farewells.

XV.

"Hey, Dad, how 'bout small inoffensive beings?
Do their feet drain this dreck? Could I render
appreciable blobs from Tiffany's striped cat
if, by the roots, I yank its ungulae
each time it comes to shit in our glassworks?"

"Assuming feline claws yield gelatin,"
he said, ambiguously, "which they don't do,
of course. Why not?"

                        Ensues a silent pause
of mutual puzzlement, during which Dad
determines it were best to clarify
conundra thus:

                        The Bradley lad should cause
our plumpish neighborette to have a birthday,
and throw a party to commemorate
first pubic floss. She'll rent a Shetland pony.

    Seducing the dwarf to the edge where the boxed-in
    gentilical Tommy is shooting his movie,
    let's stun it with swigs from our jugs of lawn toxins,
    between redwood planks mutilate its small hoofies.

    Then dole out the gooshy bits, pickled or parboiled,
    to miners of niter and leashed sunbeam doggers
    as crab apple supplements, treating the toilers,
    forfending the sit-down strike Father has augured.

The violent silent on the tube convulsed
orgasmically, showed eyeballs gouged with thumbs
and crowns cracked, egglike, with black billiard balls.
The starring maniac presumed to juggle,
incited mud fights which metastasized,
embroiling neighborhoods, recruiting scores
of terrifying people: Bradleyesque
pituitary lycanthropes.

                              "You grab
a pygmy pony footsie—"

                    "—with a snare—"

        "—contrived of plaited tendrils—"

                              "—and green twigs—"

        "—then tear the horny bits off—"

                              "—with one's teeth—"

"None left. All sacrificed for the emulsion."

Father and I are one, says sonly Christ
in Chapter Ten of his beloved disciple's
schematic gospel. Mine and his chief boy,
we banishees from Brigham's bailiwick,
in hereditary lawlessness both yoked,
are being carted off—no, galloping.

"Now hack the darling elfin tootsies free
from pinto ankles."

"Crude stone implement?"

"Dislodge a flagstone from the patio."

"Now bonk it 'gainst our domicile's foundation
until you get a jagged edge—"

"—for sawing."

"Unlay the whole array of faggy flags.
Cub Scouty charcoal gets ground underfoot.
The Nancy Boy screenplay can fuck itself."

"Language!" cries Dad, three-quarters hearted now,
a measure of paternal *oomph* restored.

While frowning dutifully, he makes a move,
ten-fingered, like an orchestral maestro
persuading tubas toward diminuendo.
The TV set cooperates, subdued.
In mud war afterglow, my grisly cuzzies
are coaxed offscreen with wads of rancid pork.
Some exposition's crudely settling in,
in preparation for the next access
of two-reel bestiality.

Dad says,
"That tiny Trigger swam here all the way
from what Brits call the Shetland Islands."

"Damn.
I never thought of that."

"You should. The Shets
(if that's their proper ethnic appellation)
look vaguely like us Cornish, possibly.
But they're subarctic, North Sea-style, as in
Ultíma Thule. Far cry from your back plot."

"Adulterative much?"

On the slim verge
of speculating, with my indoor voice,
that plumpish Tiffany's pink polished nails
perhaps might, in a useful way, resemble
homologous bits on tapirs, camels, cows,
my junior Bradley eyes engage with Senior's.
And each is well aware his counterpart
is entertaining similar, if not
identical atrociousness, or worse.
Such impermissibilities must cause
to cringe the most grotesquely retrogressed
back-tunnelized stalagmite-ducking gentiles:
Spelunkin' Tommy and his Troglo-Dad.

XVI.

So it should come as no surprise that we
edged all the way that morning, Pop and I,
to jettisoning gelatin as recourse,
on moral grounds. Byproducts of sentients
fetched in too many subtle quandaries
of, as it were, the karmic sort.

                    And glass
itself fared not much better—

                   "Hold on, son.
Let's say, for chit-chat's sake, our strident slogs
have somehow coughed up copious quanta, tons
of primo zoö-jello, quivering blobs.
The images—"

          "What images?"

                 "—are glued
to our Phoenician-style transparencies.
Their vitreousness must be remarkable,
beyond cat-shitty, bubbly, melted sand.
The flapping frame-rate's ludicrously low,
say one-point-five per second, at the most.
We've 'Pictures at an Exposition' geared
for bourgeoisie with short attention spans.
Pretend we're capable to sneak a pinch
of manganese or two. Still, any panes
the likes of us could backyard-fabricate
would, even at that snail's pace, demonstrate

a shattering propensity. We'll see
such seizured, spastic acting as will make
old Harold Lloyd look like Miss Seen Yer Heinie,
that curly-swirly skater who skims yet
through my remembered immaturity,
when I pipe-dreamt of self-expression, too."

"Glass sucks bad, pretty much, Dad, doesn't it?"

"It does, my second son."

                        Self-primed and poised
was our ex-basketballer. Time, again,
to murmur the unhallowed preparation:
outflank his odd, unreasoning aversion.
Too late, it was, in this dissolving day,
for blackmail of emotions to be needful.
Remaining cheerful, therefore, sounding frank,
eschewing pouts' manipulativeness,
I asked, the third time (triple frequency
being requisite in fairy tales, odd dreams
and edgewise jokes)—

                    "No, seriously, what *is*
the name of that plas—"

                    "Tommy, I have read
in glossy exposés that baby boomers
are not self-starters. Why, then, do you wrench
our lives like lids on jam jars, syrup-stuck?
Must you produce, direct and shoot your own?
I drive you to The Bijou, deep downtown,
whenever Disney pig-and-rat-a-ganzas
arrive to numb the Latter-Daily Saints,
or don't I?"

"—ticky stuff they use for film?"

He'd succeeded, so far, in distracting me.
But now I'd gone and uttered the F-word.
Supportive, kind and gentle, liberal,
far be it from the Treasurer, charter member
of "Neo-Zion's" own A.C.L.U.,
to micturate on Tommy's motorcade.

He gasped, or sighed. Or did he moan? I hope
my father didn't whimper, but refuse,
in any case, to show him doing so,
when from his throat he voided—

"Celluloid."

XVII.

"Our see-through-something!"

> "Are you, sonny, sure
that you've received a genuine vocation
for Motion Picture Arts and Sciences?
Will this end similar to the bassoon
now housing cobwebs, whim-wise, with the brooms,
abandoned, like your sad ham radio
and uncollected stamps-coins-baseball cards?
As I recall, you find the movies stupid."

He knew well what my future slaves must not
(especially the males among them): that,
though most emphatically no Nancy-poo,
I secretly preferred to read—except
the paperback *Swiss Family Robinson*,
a genuinely nauseating yarn,
contemptible and vile in every way.

However, back then, virgin Eves, juvie Adams,
were granted—no, force-fed, like pickled kohlrabi—
the wherewithal by means of which they, at random,
as dilettantes, languid, might fluctuate hobbies.

That year I'd already exhausted the shot put,
astronomy, macramé, ping pong, stage magic,
ventriloquization, bird watching, the sackbut,
plus dècoupage, judo, chess, crafts of the Tadzhiks.

If pyramid schemes of their kind had been running,
my pop would have mortgaged for film school tuition,
and sent me back eastward, if only this morning
I'd let him fulfill a professor's ambition.

"For celluloid I'll obviously need—"

"—some cellulose. Obtainable from trees
or frisky boychiks' cotton underpants,"
came Father's muffled words. Dejectedly,
he'd folded leg-long arms into a nest
of ostrich-size, interring his egghead.

He further moaned, "And Tommy's got to get
some ethyl alcohol. But, don't you fret.
The pyracantha berries' skins are yeasty,
their sugary pulp fermentable—unless
we burned the boughs a long, long time ago.
But you can undo that. No drinky-winky."

Then, suddenly, his massy shoulders flexed.
His face uplifted with a glimpse of hope,
as if a means to fend his phobia
had been revealed. The old man cleared his throat,
for there was an announcement to be made:

"I forgot the third ingredient," he said,
"dead requisite, if plastics, primitive,
are to be manufactured. Procurement's
a problem, given the perimeter,
parameters as well, you choose to set
so arbitrarily—"

"I never claimed
to set these -meters for myself. Not me.
Not I."

      "It won't grow here."

            "So number three's
a vegetable? Your hand's tipped."

                "Plant-derived.
And—sorry, son—as far as I can see,
the only insurmountability
that stymies your directorial debut
would be its absence, irremediable.
Not in a thousand years could this strike root
within our salted enclave."

            "Yeah? Why not?
How about a million?"

            "Given that time frame,
the backyard's groaned beneath the glacial load,
been drowned in brine, and's half-assed desert now.
But, would you stake your blossoming repute,
your future as an *artiste*, on the chance,
sweepstakes-remote, that our sixth-acre lot
resembled, ever, with sufficiency,
locales whose present longitude is rife
with orientality, where the odd tree
secreting camphor thrives? There, it's been said:
the camphor tree. And, Tommy, it is not,
in distribution, cosmopolitan.
At least, I don't believe it is—"

He stole
a glance toward the book-broom closet's warped
and bulging wooden door.

Hesitancy
on my part (learned from Pop) to dive that dumpster
encouraged his conviction: in this case,
his disbelief was not mere mis-. He felt
the sort of sweeping triumph coming on
that causes dads to wax grandiloquent.
Dismantled was the ostrich nest, and he,
with first-string center wings, up-churned our air—

"Think epiphytes, aphids, purveyors of pollen,
imagine permuted twigs, tendrils in combos,
ecology suited to nurture and burgeon
a normal tree, much less one growing in limbo—"

"And how much more so," with reluctance I whispered,
"a mutant whose whiff chases snot from one's sinus,
seed warts from one's tootsies, cold sores from one's kisser,
moth-worms from one's argyles, hemorrhoids from one's anus!"

"So, do you reckon, filmmaker-to-be,
conducements to *Cinnámomum camphora*,
with all their Far East idiosyncrasies,
in perfect concert, could at once occur
in our remotest Occident? A tad
unlikely? Flat-impossible? Gaia,
a.k.a., Mother Earth, jiggles a smidge
on her fat axis, not that much."

My pop
went out upon his aromatic limb
to sing the unavailability,

historically, of this sweet terpenoid
in our wide western hemisphere—

                    "No doubt,"
Professor Bradley lectured, "that is why
the Greeks could harness steam for toys, invent
the mighty notion of coin-op, but knew
dead zilch about—"

            He gagged upon the term,
looked at the bakelite clock cellophane-taped
upon the polyethylene wallpaper,
then said, as an aside—but not to me,
nor to himself (did Father even hear
the words?)—

            "Thank God."

                    Was he, or was he not
shifting the substantive's initial *Gee*
to upper case? (Too late to ask him now.)

  "Turn Archimedes loose with camphor wood,
let Alexandrian Heron read his notes,
and two millennia's worth of incorrupt
carcinogens would now be stifling us,
instead of merely one whole century's."

  "No shit?" our outsized juvie crowed, enthused
to press on with production now he knew
his non-biodegraded *chef-d'oeuvre*
might wreak perpetual havoc in the genome,
à la Pop's corporal non-impermanence.

"So maybe something close enough grew here,
up-sprouting anciently in our sandbox,
a stand-in for the Vapo Rub, same way
magnesium subs for manganese. Paiutes
could never be expected—well, you know."

Dad scrutinized the poison clock, again,
but this time with a different sort of face.

"Would have to've been large numbers, whole butt-loads
of years ago, a Sagan's worth of broad
millennia," my pop anachronized.

"If then," I offered.

Unexpectedly,
our four eyes met, some wisdom seeped between,
and, without further consultation, we,
in unison, came forth with—

"But, so what?"

"Time's no P-word, correct?"

"As we discussed."

"Just like that Big Whatzit you taught me true,
to take to school with monkey-cousin Darwin
for chucking in the 'Elder's' eyes like grit.
Forgot the name. Eternal Which?"

Dad said
a single, isolated amphibrach.

And, with the broach of two trisyllables,
the Big Whatzit's apotropaic hex,
positivistic posturing was shelved
and scientificality surceased.

This tonal shift was subtly paralleled
by blurrings in Mack Sennett's *mise-en-scène*.
By way of rudimentary SFX
more puffs of palm tree haze came wafting in.
Don't ask me to recount the spectacle,
dreamt beauty drifting readily from mind
across broad temporal spans like Then and Now.

XVIII.

Our suppertime had duly rolled around,
outdistanced by discolored dusk athwart
the planet's deadest dead sea, and the madman,
pranked Sanka-swilling Saint who groped the dials
of televisualism, still displayed
Mack's beauteousness, no breakfast candy ads.

Not from the minds of Dad and me had slipped,
alone, his job, but nourishment as well,
while we pursued our duel to the death.
(The second D-word's literal, as you'll tell).
Henceforth our leisured colloquy would be
a matter of materials, manifest
in my small system's spatial boundaries,
self-circumscribed, auto-imposed—for we
had shed all horological restraints
and, arm in leg-long arm, ascended toward
the realm of—

The Eternal Recurrence.

This was a further step in my "corruption"
at Father's hands, to steer me from the brink
of Brother Brig's full-dunk baptismal font.
Perdurable Reduplicativeness,
at bedtime, on flash cards, flapped in my face
as doctrine, ammo-wise, he'd issued me
for stowage in my arsenal of brain-pranks
beside the Origin of You-Know-Whats,

to fire fast salvos at that selfsame "Elder,"
the indoctrinator paid with state tax dough
to masquerade as public pedagogue.
"Eternal" such, "Recurring" this and that,
were smuggled into pseudo-science class
to tease the Saintly maniac, in case
success was met engaging him with me
on fuddlements more cosmological
than feces-flinging no-pants chimpanzees.

   Before he kicked poor Tommy out of school,
the latter naughty blasphemer enticed
the "Elder's" mind-mouth, once, almost, to sip
this bad brain coffee, percolating still
among my central nervous synapses.

   To blab it bluntly, E.R. goes like this—

   The way Jehovah, alias "Plasmator,"
would build, let's say, a car, would be to grab
the components and hurl them at a wall
again and yet again, however long
those nuts and bolts required, by accident,
to sprinkly-clink correctly into place,
resulting in a shiny spewer-forth
of oxygen and carbon atoms, paired.
Time's needed—no problem: God's well-supplied.
Assembly line efficiency aside,
your Henry Ford was not the favorite son
of this crap-shooting off-clock deity.

   Pop always drawled it out: "Gaw-w-wd the Faw-w-w-wther,"
inverting those four commas like fish hooks—
but not to bait with worms the same-named oaf

to whom the "Elder" groveled piously
in state religion class. Eternally
Recurring Oaf's no regular oaf at all,
evincing not much personality,
no appetites, pet peeves nor attributes
with which his cronies in the pantheon
still throw their weight around. And, in this way,
the Straw Boss of the E.R. might resemble
that "junior Saint next door," described by Dad,
with "steady, stubby personality."

   Along with atoms crap-shot sans surcease
against the wall came irrefutable
concomitants: my parent, the backyard,
and plumpish Tiffany with her striped cat,
and Momos, Motorolas, pyracanthas,
Phoenicians, niter, halides, celluloid,
plus flagstones with or without movie scripts
charcoaled across their quartz and feldspar—not
to mention (strange as it may sound) young me—
along with aught else you might care to bring,
recur eventually, not single times,
but bounce back yet again, an infinite
repletion of reiterated recaps,
across the course of—yes, you've guessed it right—
Eternity. For, if these nuts, those bolts,
fell into such configurations once,
whatever stops them tumbling so again?

   This jibe, old Pop assured me, beat the jeans
off Evolution as a gleeful means
to irk the angst of any Beehive Stater
with basic intellect to take it in,
the "Elder," even (maybe).

Only later
in this Hanna-Barbéra rerun known
as "life" did Tommy finally cotton on:
the same Recurring Eternality
once tickled cheerful Schiller, previous
to torturing Nietzsche. Herr Goethe's butt-boy,
and not the migraine-mustached pastor's son,
was Father's source, who, to me, passed it on—
assuming that, quite independently,
Pop never tumbled to this obviousness,
so common-sensical, once your ganglia
have been entangled in it.

Both Bradleys
assumed, much like those two fine Krauts of yore,
the process was restricted to such stuff
available at the moment, budgeted
from day the first, jumbled, yes, shuffled, but
all undestroyed, if not flat uncreated.
The "Faw-w-wther-Gaw-w-wd" is fenced in a backyard.

"So, how," one idiotically begins,
"do we know matter's limited?"—but then,
before that blather clears the tongue and teeth,
one parries one's own query with another:

> *Do you see opacity, density, leaden,*
> *between your clear corneal inlet of eyesight*
> *and Alpha Centauri, hung triply in Heaven?*
> *Made-manifest atoms are palpably finite.*

Our day was too far gone, and I too young,
to ventilate the topic, angst-irking,
of energy and matter's seamlessness,

with trendy riffs on problematic time's
duration being curtailed messily
and bent. But it was not as though the "Elder"
would be prepared, by way of refutation,
to fling these in my face, his classroom being
the hoariest of time capsules. No need
to hit the book-broom closet, arm myself
with new conceits—which tend to be no fun.

    The E. and R.'s self-similarity
was just the thing, my father thought, to drive
the Latter-Daily-Saints straight 'round the bend,
securing my expulsion, once, for all.
The Darwinistic jibes could get me damned
to brief suspensions—this was dynamite.
I, on the other hand, harbored a doubt
its oscillations furtively could wend
into my teacher's doctrine-thickened mind
with clarity, completeness, adequate
to raise one hackle on his back. Besides,
drastic results were far from guaranteed.

    It's not that much more monstrously outré
than what they know already to be true.
A tweak here, tinker there, with ease adjust
this never-ending boomerang of being
to square more tightly with the *Weltanschauung*
of our oppressors than with Prots' or Papists',
so far from Christendom is Deseret.

      If you're Brigham's fan-man and, ever so meekly,
      connubiate, fecundate moms at a bulk rate,
      and steer clear of prison while tithing biweekly
      with crisp dollar bills that your "bishop" insufflates—

—and if, through your spouses, you fetch down a whopping
contingent of souls (pre-created) from Heaven,
(if that's the broom closet they're being piled up in—
consulted, my nephew Shawn failed to enlighten)—

—and if you baptize them, full-dunk, in the Salt Church
and teach them to tithe, even though you're a gross slob,
apotheosizing awaits you, with all perks,
not merely a backyard, but your private Kolob—

—plus harems of virginal houris, upon whom
to pre-create more souls, who'll tithe till their last breath,
then, deified, whelp and tithe, ad infinitum.
(Hence Jack-Mormon Father's odd fancies of un-death.)

Take metaphors of a perpetual crap-shoot
that vividly sum up Eternal Recurrence.
Now substitute semen for crap, and the upshot
reveals "Neo-Zion's" conceptions concurrent.

   Considering his modus operandi,
it seems a tad unlikely Gaw-w-w-wd himself,
given the full recruitment of the Church
of Sanka-Sipping Saints, with all their wives,
could cough up movies on our one-sixth acre
without wiped slates, cleared decks, square-ones, ground-up,
ejaculating dice against the redwood,
spermatozoön-cubes' sextuple spots
renumbering the cosmos—at which point
the "bastard asteroid," adúmbrated
above, in Dad's foreboding senior moment,
gets shaken, cast in some fecundant nook
of our redundant solar system, thence
to swing and punch our planet off its kilter,
until, as, now, through dusk-light, Father says—

Your up's down. Your first's last. Your yammer's aphasia.
More drastic than swooping on jelliable tapirs,
the bastaroid's blasted our backyard toward Asia,
where longitudes germinate sappy snot-zappers.

"I wouldn't bank on that transpiring soon.
It's several dozen tads unlikely, not
just flat-, son, but *concave*-impossible.
We want this project brought in under-budget,
am I correct, or not? Jesus H. Christ,
instead of waiting 'round for this rogue rock
to bump us Brads behind the Bamboo Curtain,
d'you think it's slightly more efficient (time,
though not a problem, being money, still)
to grab your trike, or bike, whatever, roll
until you bonk against the pharmacy
and buy a box of fucking camphor?"

                              "No.
That stuff is shelved with prophylactics, aspirin,
mascara, candy—all adulterants."

  "I'd dig to front you bread, man."

                         (In crises,
my Pop would inauthentically abuse
such TV beatnik lingo, to persuade.
It worked on Older Sibling, briefly, half
a decade gone.)

              "Fuck that," I said. "In fact,
fuck *it*, entire."

              I feinted toward my room,
again, and its sweet tubes of airplane glue.

XIX.

Congenital, barely considered, pre-wired
impulses told me, "Tommy, if you would bother
to rise from your Bradley ass, as though inspired,
spelunk yourself, excavate something or other—"

—(which delving's no part of survival's smooth struggle
in prosperous times like my long prepubescence,
when even us infidels, massively huddled
in Deseret, if white, were owed an existence)—

"—but make it ex nihilo, Edenic, no shoulders
of giants, no optometristic fire lighters,
no outfitters, midwives, no pimps, no coat-holders.
Collaborative art is for Nancy screenwriters.

"Your gr'auntie vocabulized, grammared her patter
among the stalagmites, a thousand miles distant
from dining cars bustling with casual chatters,
two thousand beyond Walden's yammering piss-ant.

"So why blow your energy/matter on artwork
that needs a cómplex, military-industrial,
backed up by a world-wide distributor network,
to gather constituents, basic materials?"

Decorum, grace, taste, discipline demand
strict circumscription of topography,
no alienness, no extraneity.
One requisite for making film for films

was elsewhere to be had, just down the block.
The protoplanetary hand of iron
and nickel that could push the drugstore near
was not exactly waving in the sky.

On this as yet undwindled day—though Dad
and I were unaware (or dimly so)—
our backyard was the topiaried soul,
unsmutched and prelapsarian, the self's
walled garden, round yet quadrilateral.
Back to white wilderness I'd sooner see
this 'burb revert, resolved to alkali,
than let my blossom-bower be trespassed
upon and rendered maculate—or not?
Was my most recent failure to "watch language,"
my second exhortation, to the effect
that *it*, roundly, summarily, be *fucked*,
a *cri de coeur* or flim-flam?

Not alone
would Bradley, Jr., be in acquiescing.
Senior himself, apparently, thought time
for *it-fucking* had finally arrived.
As if to speed my roomward skulk, Dad said—

> *You've problems: your glass plates will shatter; and, sadly,*
> *your celluloid's likely as Saints with few cousins.*
> *Your premiere's postponed till the cosmos ends badly,*
> *if time can climax, which, recurring, it doesn't.*

"The production, Tommy, seems to've hit a wall,
and never's bouncing back all of a piece,
regardless of how numerous the cracks
your not-so-little skull sustains on bricks.

No magic moments from the silver screen,
nor even slabs of darksome bark, today,
in Salt Lake's glitzless 'burbs. Such stoppages
of his resplendent muse dogged Orson Welles,
who learned card tricks and got on with his life.
And he's been hailed, by critics from back east,
as an authentic genius.

          "Can I go
to work now? Almost time to undertake
the hectic commute home, if I intend
to grab my normal jump on rush hour, wend
my way back to our domicile, here spend
what child behaviorists warmly extol
as 'quality time,' pre-beddy-bye, with you,
my second son, as wholesome fathers ought.
Goom-bye, please?"

          Swamped with negativity,
with Father, the whole Universe as well,
refusing to cooperate, did one
dig deep into oneself and, valiantly,
find wherewithal, somehow, to persevere?
You know one did. It's what they signify
who sing of "youth's tenacity."

          My turn
to do the buttonholing. Just as Dad
was bending at the waist to clear the lintel,
I blocked, this time with plucky face alone,
our ex-pro basketballer—all the more
impressively as it was dark, light bulbs
by neither Bradley having been switched on.
Emulsions, hairline-cracked, patched, flickering,

transmogged to pixels' primitive gray glimmer,
were all we had for mutual scrutiny.

   Congenital subnormals, earlier lured
offscreen with putrid pork, have been allowed
back into frame. They're vaguely organized.
Contingents of pituitary goons,
all Bradleyesque, are on the shambling verge
of gaining upper hands. They recommence
the mud fight, escalating with a grunt
to broken bottles, stones.

          "The asteroid belt's
a flying Rocky Mountain range," I say.
"It's only, so to speak, a matter of—"

          Dad
regards me for an indeterminate while.
And then, with all the grim reluctance shown
by generals, five-starred, who've always known
when to go nuclear, he sets him down.

XX.

"For large segments of geologic time
we've loitered in the sandbox. Yahweh's sap
has, as expected, handily swung by,
subcranially concussing us. Your east
has met your west, your left your right. Meanwhile,
wonder of wonders! God damn! Can you guess
what grows in our backyard? *Cinnámomum
camphora*! We've a forest and a half
of nasal decongestant, bags and bags
of stuff that's plasticky, more than enough
luxuriantly to shoot eight dozen sequels,
or more, to *Lawrence of Arabia*.
Now, are you ready, boy, or are you not,
to field the hardest question of them all?"

I flipped my Beatle bangs out of my eyes,
and sat up straight.

        The Motorola mocked,
meantime, a house, two-storied, being razed
bare-handedly by one Gargantua,
his face lopsided.

        "What about," asked Dad,
"your actors?"

        Wait. Do I, maybe, recall
once coming home from state religion class
and guilelessly inquiring of this man

how annex Kolobs get pre-populated,
the "Elder" having dodged the smutty details?
Had Dad demurred, as well, or taught me true
of Birds, of Bees, of Rubbers (sturdy latex,
though plasticky they be, and incorrupt—
none of this ungulate intestine tripe)?
The wisdom, as received in days gone by,
prescribed postponing that hygienic speech
until the progeny began to stink.
That moment of malodor signaled, too,
the time for novice dating to commence,
if tentatively. Tommy still reeked sweet,
I'm pretty sure—though my retentive powers,
olfactory, cannot, blindfolded, claim
the rehashed sharpness of Proust's gustatory,
for Pop's son was no Nancified nib-licker.
(That can't be emphasized too frequently.)

    In any case, how ill-prepared was I
for Daddy's "hardest question of them all,"
believing Lassie was a boy, Bambi
his opposite? While "borderline precocious"
in one department, your narrator-lad
remained a cipher, in mid-latency,
pre-genitalic—if you want to wax
all psychoanalytical—thus doomed,
if things went well, to supersession, death
by adolescence. Not to sugar-coat:
I'd not yet started "beating out the brains
of Charles the Bald," as Gauls like Derrida
and Foucault do, and say, by way of proverb.
But, most reluctantly, I'd overheard
the miniature polygamists at school
spout naughty talk, and wasn't hankering

to be subjected further, in my house,
by Father, yet. For *ick*.

         "My actors? Well—"
(An innocence, part feigned, informed my tone,
half-consciously attempting to deflect
paternal will and impulse.) "—apples, crab.
They'll chow with slaves."

            "You know I don't refer
to commissary privileges, boy.
The Holy Grail, I've heard, in Hollywood,
is—what's the phrase? Artistic Which?"

                "Control."

   "That's what you want, correct? It might be had
in indie Deseret."

        "Um, gee-whiz, Dad.
I never, honestly—"

        Mouth balked, I looked
to Sennett for support, the moral sort,
and saw great aunties, cuzzies thrice removed,
hyperextended, botched. If eugenics
can be considered artistry, control
was not exerted on their beingness.

> *Directors display their souls via performers.*
> *Think Ingmar on Fårö with Liv and von Sydow.*
> *If willing to allocate space, just one corner,*
> *you, too, can exhibit your spirit, but more so.*

We'll cause a small twig-and-green-tendril deployment,
a lean-to, for privacy, and, with sufficient
technique, qualitatively manage employees'
genetic expressions, sublime or deficient.

The cheekbones, the irises (preferably turquoise),
the muscles, or lack thereof—even, depending
on Nature and Nurture, the pert girls, the curt boys
can gestate the psyches your screenplay's demanding.

"There is a script?

       "What? Yes. As we discussed."

"I thought the flagstones got dislodged, unlaid."

"I gathered them back up."

       "Did we decide
to grind the charcoal underfoot?"

       "Gathered,
as well, back up."

       "I see," said Father.

       This
is getting altogether too heuristic.
It's Tommy Bradley's turn, now, to demur,
to put the brakes on, introduce restraints,
persuade, admonish Trigger to "Whoa back,"
step off a bit, gain distance, scribble down
preliminary slug-lines, dialogue,
establish shots of where we're headed, prior

to zooming in. Make like Phoenicians,
engage the alphabet, effeminate
though it may seem, to some, to be, before
we churn out body fluids by the quart.
(Did someone say *byproducts of sentients*?)

    The pre-teen clears his throat and whispers, "Pop?
How much time are we looking at?"

                    "Who cares?
It's Mormon Heaven now, and you're the boss.
It's your planet, your Kolob, we're peopling."

XXI.

Genetic engineering, in those years,
had yet to ooze, grim, sticky, from the pulp
of trashy novelettes and into labs.
In any case, it's doubtful whether I,
from Father's modest rear plot's sediment,
could scratch and scrounge the Frankensteinian gear:
the boric oxide for our pyrex beakers
and petri dishes, where fake babies sprout
in agar-agar (wrung from rank seaweed,
a rare commodity in "Neo-Zion,"
as our sea's dead to all biology).
Y-chromosomal both, we had no choice
but that most uninventive of recourses:
selective breeding, primitive, heuristic.

Spelunkin' Tommy now got Troglo-Dad's
aforesaid cryptic comment with regard
to "jobs of work for plumpish Tiffany."
His other gauzy utterance, as well,
had, up till now, remained un-cottoned onto,
about the "punters' population pool
occurring naturally." It seems recruits,
aesthetically selected from amongst
my niter-miners and my hut-rotators,
those "friends," illegals, who had climbed the fence,
those—not wet-, but *dry*-backs—must whelp my cast
of anchor-baby Oscar nominees.

The thought was off-putting. Therefore, our lad,
our persevering, most tenacious youth,
unearthed, all by himself, the only dead
insuperability, sole stumbling block,
that hampered hopes of homespun Hollywood.
And what would such a stubborn stymie be?
It would be Dad's sick-making prank, or scheme,
of, in the backyard, people doing *it*
behind some twigs and tendrils. Intercourse
with girls. Gross. Cooties.

                  It occurred to me
much later, in "adulthood," so to speak
(a minute and a half ago, in fact),
to wonder if my hard-won celluloid
appealed to Daddy as preservative
for, as it were, posterity: to film
hyperfecundant spawn of Brigham Young
in conjugation, writhing, grunting up
the blue-eyed heartthrobs, comely ingénues,
by way of whose enticing superficies
my "soul" was scripted for "display."

                     Old perv.
Perhaps some other crap-shot, bounced-back time,
when Film Advisory Boards have not recurred.

He did, however, have a solid point,
one not to be ignored. My thespians
would play my Shadow, Animus and Self
(also that other "aspect" on the roster,
the fourth component of one's mental innards,
whose nomenclature slips my mind today):

all interblended partial Tommy Bradleys,
each from the others teased apart, assigned
a carcass and a part to play, in plots
that mingle kids for dramatizing truths
about essential *me*, exhibit A,
as screened before the bench of cosmic "Elder"
in pleas for readmission.

                   How allow
the very lineaments of my dramatis
personae, which foregoing rigmaroles
were essayed to emulsify, be draped
on Latter-Daily bones—unpedigreed,
miscegenated menials, multi-mommed,
adulterative redwood-scaling brats,
promiscuous trespassers, sunburnt, blond
as any spastic slapstick clown—absent
a twig-and-tendril modicum, at least,
of, so to speak, unnatural selection?

  Besides which (not to change the subject, much),
I was determined Dad not repossess
my baby teeth, nor garner my gonads,
nor misconstrue *auteur*'s integrity
as homo-squeamishness, nor misassume
his son to be a Nancy invert-sugar.

  So, fighting back the nauseous vertigo
of first erotic flusterment, one chokes
and hiccoughs, bravely, this octet of words:

  "Okay. Let's pick green twigs for that lean-to."

XXII.

To which there's no reply but blinks. Dad thought
he had me, this time, by the bicuspids,
already inventorying the fillings,
like Bergen-Belsen's oral hygienist.

"We're talking serial parturition here,"
he cautions me unnecessarily,
a tinge of desperation in his tone.
A full day's honest work's already trashed.
It follows something else must make him twitch
with urges, all too evident, to dive,
head-first, through our front door.

                       Discomfiture
aside, he's much too canny to inquire,
outright, if my enthusiasm's curbed
by multi-generationality.
No wronger question can be put to boys,
American, whole-blood, no special needs,
no learning disabilities with pills,
no deviancies diagnosed, just yet,
for here's the answer you're liable to get:

"Like you, I am immortal, Pop. It runs,
recessive gene-wise, in the family,
like ginger coloration. Time's no prob."

And yet, of course, in spite of my brave stance,
asseveration's heartiness aside,
upon the point of death this morbid tyke's

been semi-consciously impaled all day—
a paradox in view of his sparse years.
And maybe Dad, sky hook Prometheus,
is, also, at his no less tender age
(contrary protestations notwithstanding),
enchanted by that coming climax, when
the things that can't be taken when you go—

    —are gone, and you're exiled, stalagmites up-propping
    your bier, and your gr'aunties and siblings-cum-cousins
    with crypto-talk eulogize. Meanwhile they're slopping
    your face with brown bat fat, extremest of unctions.

    Collateral Bradley-goons Mack Sennett's granted
    compassionate leave to attend your off-soaring,
    anachronist-atavist hymns being grunted,
    are coveting throwable stones on the flooring.

    The grizzlies and timber wolves, anti-crèche livestock,
    are poking through fissures their muzzles and blunt fangs
    to nip counter-Christ in his manger of bedrock
    and snarl along rhythmically with his un-birth pangs.

    Autonomous hypothalamical nerve-throbs
    afford you small help, then no help, then cold hindrance
    as auricles, ventricles, bronchi and lung-lobes
    make doomed declarations of gasped independence.

    Why was this relict Cornishman prepared
to excavate our mere sixth-acre plot
as if it were a tunnel shot with tin?
He sought that buried system, self-sustained,
embodied briefly in the microcosm
at personhood's end-time. He scraped and chipped

at his own cranium's blackened inner wall
for disengagement and demise: that point
where plumpish Tiffany's irrelevant
as time. The child is father to the man,
the pre-teen forebear to the corpse.

                       I scrounged
back there for sheer autonomy, sole boon
for gentiles reft of planetary sway,
that comes with death's precision—only then:
our half-blink of neat freedom, mortal coil
successfully off-shuffled, once, for all,
subséquent to a finished life of squirms.
It lasts, this liberation, say, how long:
a single flick's immensurate duration,
a short-short subject, lit by half a pinch
of volatile magnesium, wrung from weeds.

XXIII.

My father, the "immortal," self-proclaimed,
wound up surprised, eight months ago, to gain
that fleeting liberty, as you well knew
our scheduling restraints would make him do—
eventually real boys must off their pops.
Succumbing to his urge to dive, head-first,
through our front door, Dad whispered, "Goom-bye, please,"
and left my teeth, my testicles to me,
forfeiting, thus, his life. To that old soul
farewells were fondly bid, as usual.
The young man and/or large lad's tendency
is liquidating Laius.

Just a means
of bumping Dada off, this poem of mine,
my patricide-by-Nancy charcoal scrawl.
I did it, and you watched. Throughout these stichs,
verse paragraphs and amphibrachic quatrains,
I rendered him a snickering maniac,
a breakfast table ditherer in the dark,
an incoherent yammerer of jibes
about a backyard jail bait stud farm, job
ripped from his grasp—which is as much to say
I murdered Pappy in the only way
that counts. And, till the canto previous,
the Unities, "Aristotelian,"
were well preserved.

"Real primitivity,
à la Swiss Families, we've conjured, son,"
he says to me at night when, fitfully,
before the small screen I attempt to snore.
"Gray umbras, negatives upon cave walls,
doomed for a certain term—that sort of thing."

XXIV.

Astronomers scope exoplanet environs
as chemical dump sites, where Latter-Day landlords
on barren rock replay misdoings of Onan,
perpetually spilling their Brigham-sized splooge-loads.

If this solar ghetto's grim Kolobs are bona fide,
the spheroids elsewhere which the cosmos unlooses
ooze acid for rainfall and waft nitrous oxide
for gaseously laughing at dads' self-abuses.

A wretch of an alien worm, microscopic,
more mud-ball than courier of karma, our cousin,
our extraterrestrial hope, squalid, toxic,
proves we're not alone, in galactic quintillions.

That's how many dice must rebound off our Gaw-wd's wall,
with limited atoms, unlimited schedule,
to conjure what's coiling in back of my eyeballs
and sizzling between both my Bradleyesque ear-holes.

No matter how tedious our crap-shooter Faw-w-w-wther
found tossing me, he'd never trike to the drugstore
for boxes of Tommy ingredients. He'd bother
no sooner than I'd fetch adulterative camphor.

However, I, moments ago, without
the book-broom closet's aid, but Google's, learned
snot-zapper trees from Mao Land do, indeed,
thrive in our broad, proud honky hemisphere.

Dad's dis- was misbelief, as it turns out.
A century past they were imported—or,
perhaps, *exiled*'s a better term—upon
the heels, hyperextended, of a clan
of Cornish tin miners. And they (the trees,
not we) now multiply like sandbox weeds,
to drastic detriment of native greens.
Cinnámomum camphora, un-harássed
by predators, chokes forests, shoves aside
slim saplings for its selfish ends and means.
Brought over as a garden ornament,
it's now despised, feared, registered amongst
invasive species, not to be condoned.

Just such a pest, in fact and unbeknownst
to Bradleys (neither being a botanist),
up-sprouted rankly some few feet beyond
our plumpish Tiffany's crab apple tree.
(Sciento-blunder worthy of Golding.)
Had Daddy's "bastaroid" nudged, after all,
my studio—mere glancing blow, sideswipe,
sub-Richter scale—World Cinema would glow
with Tommy's contribution. Ill-informed
parental misguidance, groundless and glib,
caused wastage irrecoverable, deep loss
immeasurable to humankind. Besides,
stale turpentine would work as well, I'm told.
(A can was stashed behind the Frigidaire.)

But, on that day of youth, which won't recur
(not this specific time around), the third
ingredient's unavailability
was taught me false, as insurmountable.

Emulsion hence eschewed, I bent my gaze
toward title cards and, watching language, said,
"Fuck it," skulked off, turned scribbler-boy, instead.

XXV.

I waxed Phoenician, baptized me full-dunk
in Nancy's alphabet. And, with that stroke
of will, the technical perplexities
discussed in Cantos One through Twenty-Two,
above, were obviated.

               I admit
to having not a clue whence comes the graphite
that charges my Ticonderoga. But
it could, with extra effort, be, instead,
charcoal from Dad's reviled black locusts—if
those trash trees had to aphids not succumbed
and rotted off to Kolob, powdered ghosts,
with nary twig nor tendril left to roast.

So now one pencils long poems, not about
a boy and his old pop who try to ape
life's overflow with light in a backyard,
but rather two odd stumblers, Cornishmen,
resembling us as predecessors will,
gigantic gingers, wandering the length
and unfenced breadth of Earth, millennia prior
to pictures made with anything but hands
plus pigments on a surface, stable, still.
Research, guffawing, this "creative's" done
with books in every bookish substance bound,
and fetched, uncloseted, from everywhere.

My father's final words were not death-rattled,
but crooned: "I'm checkin' out, goom-bye." Before
he managed that, guess whose adhesive thumb
was laid athwart his *carte de bibliothèque*
to pull some *checkin'-out, goom-byeing*, too.

Two hundred tomes transgressed the broad Pacific,
absconded with, in suitcases, away,
to longitudes of camphor trees, where, now,
subséquent to grown Tommy's second exile,
suspended by oppressors from his place
of banished Bradley birth, he languishes,
with books enough to bury, up to chins,
twelve tribes of strange pituitary goons
and private lingo-blabbing great-great aunties.

Sunk, steeped in orientality, spelunked
yet deeper down ejectees' bleak mineshaft,
this heathen's snagged no Deseret career.
My dad's program of son-corruption far
outflew his bitter plan. Expatriate,
I'm *too* unsocialized by standards set
by commies, rummies, free-verse pederasts
at Pop's non-Mormon university.

Revenge upon that clip joint's musty stacks
was wreaked by cackling Tommy. How? By means
of Interlibrary Loan. I put vast piles,
volumes of silverfishy pagination,
upon my old man's faculty account,
who, in the meantime, croaked.

My rival sibling,
playhouse collaborator, has announced
to all of "Neo-Zion" that a notice,
up-reckoning of "Items Overdue,"
exploded Pop's heart gaskets with sheer shock—
a gross distortion of my paper trail,
impugning Tommy's conscientiousness,
his good comportment, as a co-survivor
of our professor pater.

I confess—

—to've larcenized titles from Bombay, from Belgium,
from Boise Vocational College, and now from
a disparate century, brand-new millennium
(if one ignores Dennis the Lesser's conundrum).

Gaw-wd knows what glues, cotton bonds, inkings that glisten,
what larvae-rife sizing, what dyes, artificial,
I've brought to pollute the porous ecosystem
of my bamboo Kolob, my rice-reeking hovel.

—but, though one's Sino-hosts say, "Stealing books
is not stealing," one's filial piety
(Confucian, lately learned) precludes accrual
of astronomic fines, compounded, tallied
against Dad's patronymic (and his offspring's)
on that Great Karmic Debit Sheet, up yonder.
In spite of what the other Bradley snipes,
these babies' check-out status gets re-upped
bimonthly, if transoceanically,
by means of fax machinery, our pop's
own reverend, immemorial honorific
ballpointed on the page, immutable,
beside his S.S.N. (hijacked by me).

The date, one half a dozen times per year,
must be adjusted, hand-scrawled by this poet,
upon another leprous layer, thicker,
increasingly opaque and crusty, of
the store-bought product trademarked Liquid Paper,
manufactured up the road in old Shanghai.
Composed of mustard oil and lampblack, both
Swiss Family-doable, it might sit well,
if not commixed with these adulterants
that, in the Middle Kingdom's hieroglyphs,
through myriads of bristling ideographs,
twing-twang at me, unalphabetically,
fine-printed, from the mini-bottle's label:

> *Methylcyclohéxane mulled with isobutyl*
> *methácrylate, plus a soupçon of titanium*
> *dioxide sulfósuccinate, which is brutal,*
> *and vinyl copolymers, shaming to name 'em.*

This Date Line trespasser's meandered far
from prepubescent boychik fantasies
of building him a pure economy
in emulation of his virgin forebears,
whose femurs grew stalagmite-strong in caves.
He must import such outré essences,
quintessences, exotic, plasticky,
to get his world researched and blankly versed.

> *I personally cause, every eighth week, a quantum*
> *upsurge in world usage of pentaerythrítol,*
> *of phthalates, of alkyds, of dioctyl sodium,*
> *and, worst of all, cyclohexa-nedimethanol.*

Hermetic ambitions of closure fast fading,
promiscuous tastes for strange substances pandered,
the library's dun-sheet for check-out updating
can barely be crammed in facsimile scanners.

Technology, dated, 'tard-simple in principle
(in real anti-Nancy boys' backyards so plenteous,
snot, also, can blot out), exposes my multiple
addiction, adulterative, if not adulterous.

XXVI.

By externalities we don't remain
long unsustained. We have (or need to think
we have) a victualler-pop, perpetual.
To execute the narcissistic plan
informing this *Künstlerroman*, I quelled
my weeps just long enough to fudge a smidge
upon my bounteous caterer's "checkin' out,
goom-byeing" to non-perpetuity.

In order that the Liquid Paper's swell
should crust enough to render plausible
this thick conceit that, metaphysically,
rounds off my autohagiography,
I must accomplish Pop's demise before
the fortnight whose sad denouement, today,
commemorates, with fair solemnity,
death's semi-monthly anniversary.
It's either that or flagrantly abuse
the narrator's prerogative to fib,
and cause the gentiles' drab diploma mill's
circúlatory fascists to demand
renewal faxes at ungodly rates:
say, every pettily pacing business day.

I can encompass and re-schedule kills
of minor sports figures, sky hookers, but
prove impotent arresting my descent
to techno-whoredom. Alkyds and phthalates,
copolymers of vinyl, methacrylates,

spread but a superficial epiderm
on my corrupted Karloff-carcass.

                    Let
us shudder, now, to hear what's been required
to bring these six and twenty metric cantos
before your eyeballs, simply pencil-traced
though in their pristine state they might've been:
the interlinkage of contrivances
no boy, regardless of how "borderline"
his own "precocity," could scrounge from scratch,
nor broad his backyard bourne, with all its plants
and minerals, nor tractable his slaves,
nor patient and indulgent his old man:

> *The voicemail to which these stanzas were entrusted*
> *behaved in ways unsynched with New Zionism.*
> *Account has been taken, its schedule adjusted*
> *for Einstein's slick temporal relativism.*
>
> *It bounced off two satellites over the ocean,*
> *light-speeding, careening, like girls doing ass-twerks,*
> *caused* tempus *to* fugit, *to skulk in slow motion,*
> *at frame-rates more suited to sandboxes' glassworks.*
>
> *On Mormondom's mountainous outskirts these quatrains*
> *descended tardy, just a smidge, though the business*
> *was instantaneous. (Ponder that with a boy's brain*
> *retarded by Swiss Family primitiveness.)*

    To compensate for planetary spin
that we, but not my verses, meantime spun,
the receiver (dish? antenna? take your pick)
was nudged, judiciously, a semi-skosh,

due west, toward my Asiatic modem.
Precisely single digits' worth of inches,
or maybe millimeters, it was coaxed,
to verge the cavern-riddled sheer cliff-edge
of a fourteen-thousand-foot-high prominence,
across whose quartz and feldspar face, I'm told,
a certain urn of academic ash
is scheduled to be dumped, like dialogue
and slug lines on a flagstone page charcoaled.
Much like this book, Dad's flying home to Gr'Auntie.

   To keep my penta- and tetrameters
from swishing past you in your Deseret,
the recently enfeebled fourth dimension's
indulged in all its idiosyncrasies,
its dilatory whims anticipated.
And thus is illegitimized the sole
assumption that forestalled the shutting down
of my production, prior to missing lunch.
It turns out, after all, that time is not
imbued with unproblematicity.

   My final act of unfiliality,
of Dad-betrayal, isn't patricide,
but practical negation of the doctrine
he taught me for self-preservation's sake.
How can one's eternality, uninjured,
recur when, in the meanwhile, time's compressed
and stretched, substandard animal jelly-wise?
Eternity itself's non-sequitur,
"recurrence" oxymoron, when the fence
that segregates Then, Now and Soon gets burnt.

So Tommy's left without a secret weapon
against the "Elders" of this world. He might
as well, if not prodigiously whelp brats
on supernumerary wives, then tithe,
kiss ten percent of his moolah goom-bye,
Cathayan *renminbi* although it be;
backslide like Shawnster; sidle up, discreet,
to Mo-Mo missionaries, two by two,
the fraudulently visaed hometown boys
who troll for dupes through China's backmost streets.
They'll bring him, baptized, full-dunk, to the cult
that nigh expunged us Bradleys, time ago.

Against that ultimate succumbing, one's
Ticonderoga's whittled to degrees
that may appear compulsive, till the point
where one's enthusiasms scrape the page
is circumscribed, near-geometrically:
a contact to be severed painlessly
when time for disengagement has arrived,
do-it-oneself-sufficiency achieved.

Other Books by Tom Bradley

POETRY

Nagasaki Soul Huffer:
a Manhunt in Fifty-Five Cantos

Energeticum / Phantasticum:
a Profane Epyllion in Seven Cantos

Useful Despair
as Taught to the Hemorrhaging Slave
of an Obese Eunuch
(illustrated by Nick Patterson)

We'll See Who Seduces Whom: a Graphic Ekphrasis in Verse
(illustrated by David Aronson)

NONFICTION

Put It Down in a Book

Fission Among the Fanatics

New Cross-Fucked Musings on a Manic Reality

SCREENPLAYS

Three Screenplays

SHORT STORIES

Hemorrhaging Slave of an Obese Eunuch

*A Pleasure Jaunt With One of the Sex Workers
Who Don't Exist in the People's Republic of China*

Calliope's Boy

Even the Dog Won't Touch Me

NOVELS

Elmer Crowley: a Katabasic Nekyia
(illustrated by Nick Patterson and David Aronson)

Family Romance
(illustrated by Nick Patterson)

Felicia's Nose
(with Carol Novack, illustrated by Nick Patterson)

This Wasted Land
(with Marc Vincenz)

The Church of Latter-Day Eugenics
(with Chris Kelso)

Epigonesia
(with Kane X. Faucher)

My Hands Were Clean

Breakfast With Streckfuss

Vital Fluid

Hustling the East

Kara-kun, Flip-kun:
Two Hiroshima Tales

Black Class Cur

Acting Alone:
a Novel of Nuns, Neo-Nazis and NORAD

Bomb Baby

Lemur

The Curved Jewels

Killing Bryce

tombradley.org

Printed in January 2020
by Gauvin Press,
Gatineau, Québec